2024 LUXEMBOURG TRAVEL GUIDE

The Ultimate Guide to The Best Adventure, Top Attractions, Tourist Spots, Architecture, Landscapes, History, Culture, Cuisine, Tips and Local Secrets for Your Perfect Trip.

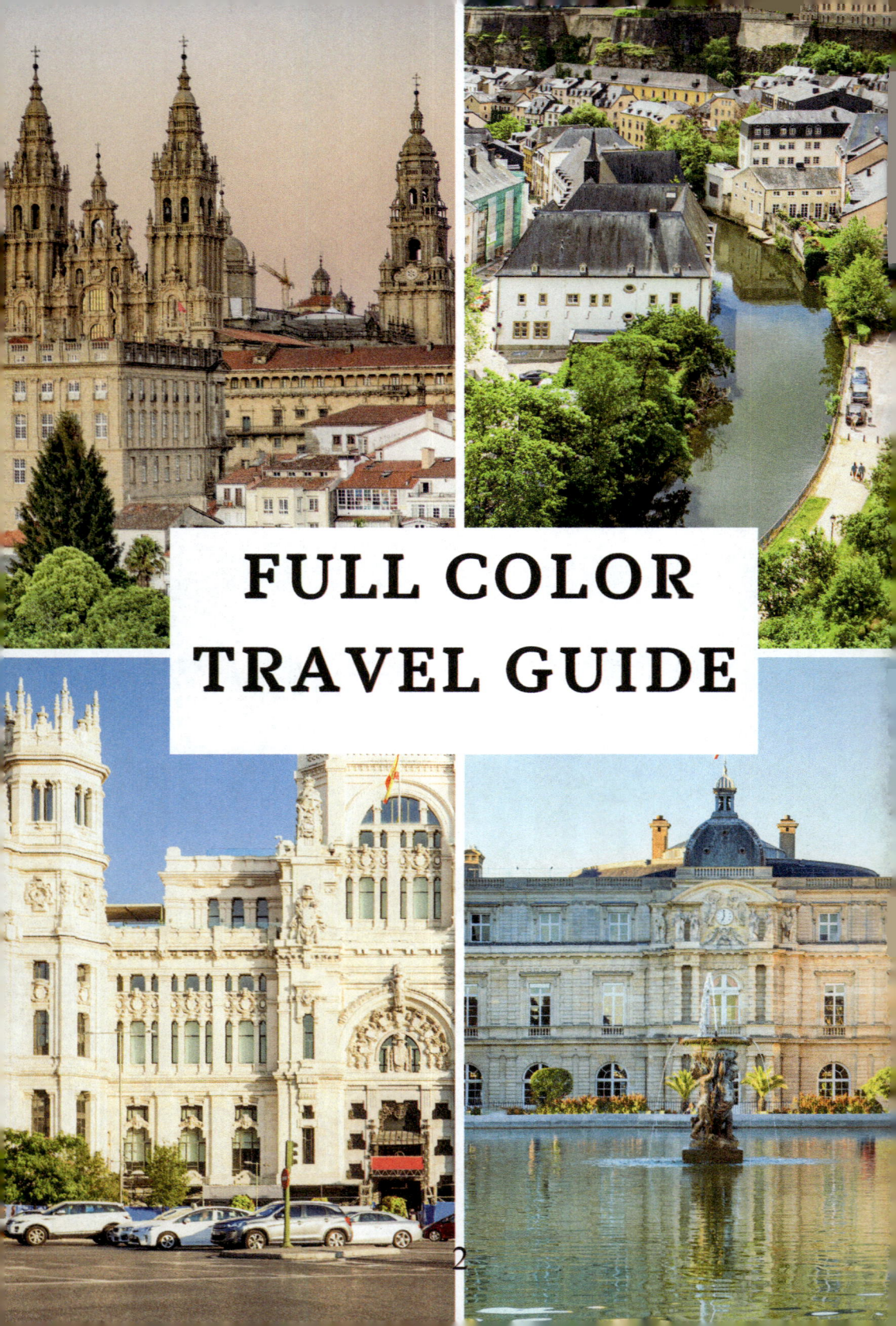

FULL COLOR TRAVEL GUIDE

(Christopher Kibler), (2024)
All rights reserved. This book is written by Christopher Kibler.
No part of this publication may be reproduced, distributed, or transmitted in any form or by any means, including photocopying, recording, or other electronic or mechanical methods, without the prior written permission of the publisher, except in the case of brief quotations embodied in critical reviews and certain other non-commercial uses permitted by copyright law.

Luxembourg City Map

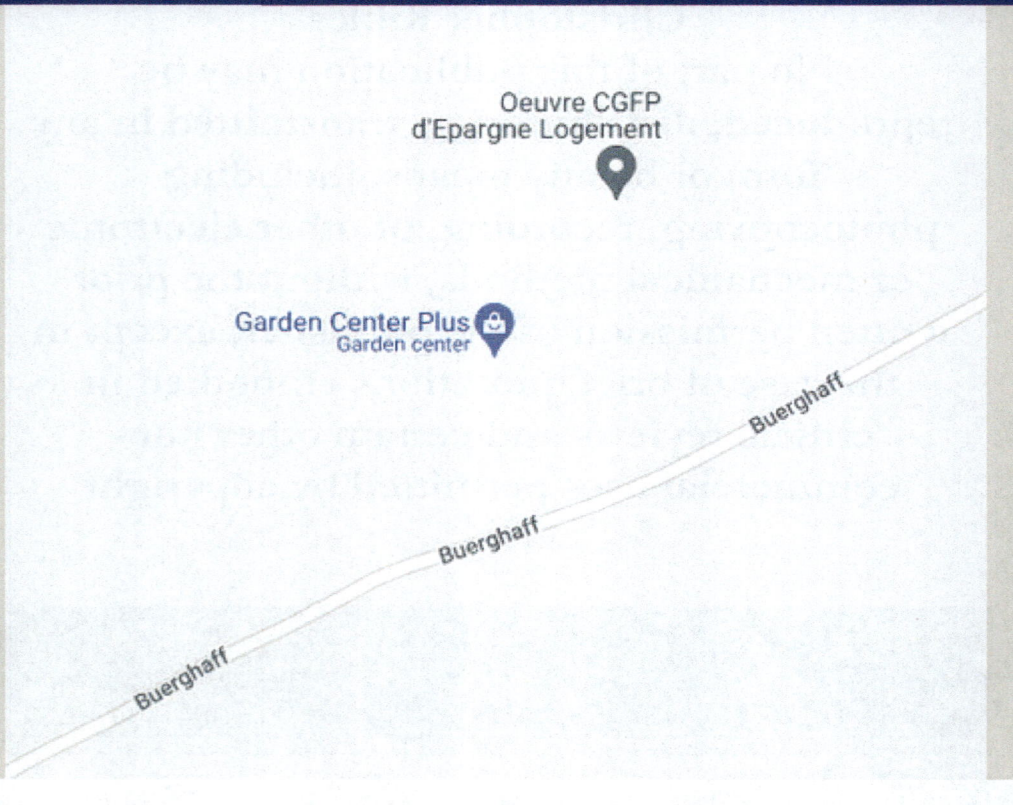

SCAN THE QR CODE

1. Open your device camera app.
2. Point the camera at the QR code.
3. Ensure the QR code is within the frame and well-lit.
4. Wait for your device to recognize the Qr code.
5. Once recognized, tap on the notification or follow the prompt to access the content or action associated with the QR code.

4

ABOUT THE AUTHOR

Meet Christopher Kibler, the audacious spirit and writer behind captivating travel guidebooks. Christopher Kibler, isn't only an author but also a seasoned traveler who can't get enough of the world's wonders.

He takes readers on a journey of discovery with every page, guiding them to the furthest corners of the earth.

Traveling is more than just a hobby for Christopher; it is ingrained in his very being, and his work demonstrates the excitement and authenticity that each locale brings.

His guides offer readers a taste of city life in vibrant metropolises and the serene solitude of untouched landscapes.

The author meticulously researches every aspect of a destination, offering readers the best-kept secrets and advice,

Come along and explore the globe with him, where he'll guide you through the enchanting power of travel, uncovering the wonders of each place, step by step.

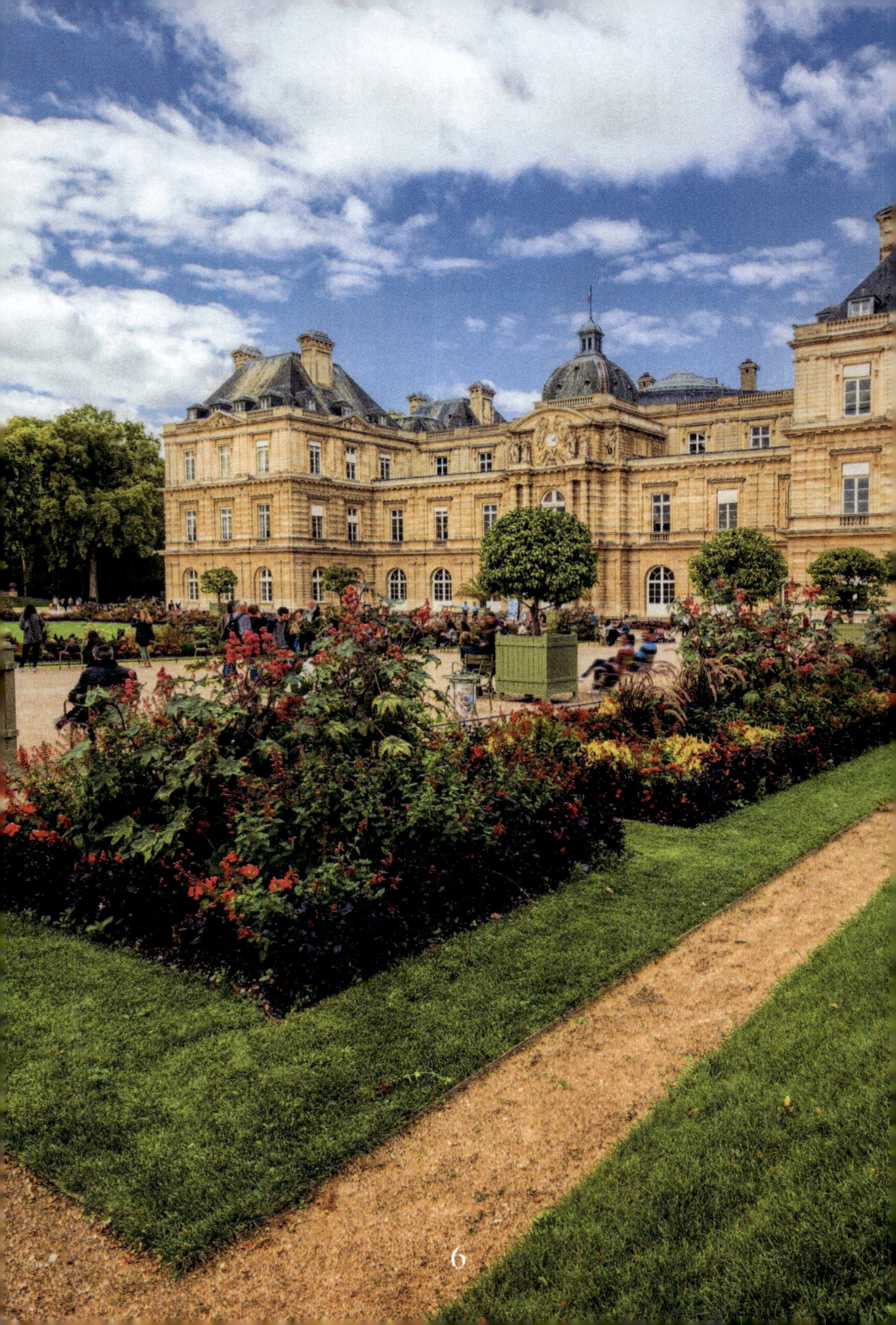

TABLE OF CONTENT

INTRODUCTION 11

Top reasons to go to Luxembourg in 2024............15
Facts about Luxembourg 17
Basic communication words to use when you travel..19
Abbrevations and codes...23
Resturant price codes...25

ABOUT LUXEMBOURG...27

History 30
Geography and Climate 33
Government and Politics 36
Laws..38
People and Culture...41
Language and Religion 48

PRATICAL INFORMATION.....47

Visa Requirements and Documents......................48
Currency and Rate of Exchange............................51
Cultural etiquette...52
International Telephone and useful Telephone Numbers...54
Travel Costs to Luxembourg estimated in Budget-friendly, Mid range and Luxury..............................55
Time and Electricity...58
Transportation Options To and Within Luxembourg...60
International Flights and Major Airports.............64

PLANNING YOUR TRIP....67

Travel Essentials... 68
When to Visit and the best time to visit................70
Safety Precautions and Instruments.....................72
Electronics and gadget 75
Mobile apps 77
Itinerary..80

ACCOMDATION......83

Hostels..84
Campgrounds...89
Affordable and Budget-Friendly hotels.................94
Luxury Hotels...100
Family Hotels...107
Romatic Hotels..114

EXPLORING LEUXEMBOURG 121

Tours and activities (Walking, Buses, cycling and wine tasting tours)..122
Top Attractions..131
Iconic sites and Land marks 140
Museums / Hidden gems....................................147
Nature and Parks 155
Fun and Games...163
Nightlife Activities...167
Spas and Wellness 172
Shows and Concert activities.............................177

RESTAURANTS......183

Local cuisine..184
Fine dining/Romantic..190
Budget friendly 196
Coffe and tea..205
Bars and Pubs 210

SHOPPING 215

Shopping Malls/ Gift Shops..216
Local Markets..222

EVENTS.....227

Public holidays..228
National day celebrations 229
Festivals 231

MAPS........241

CONCLUSION......245

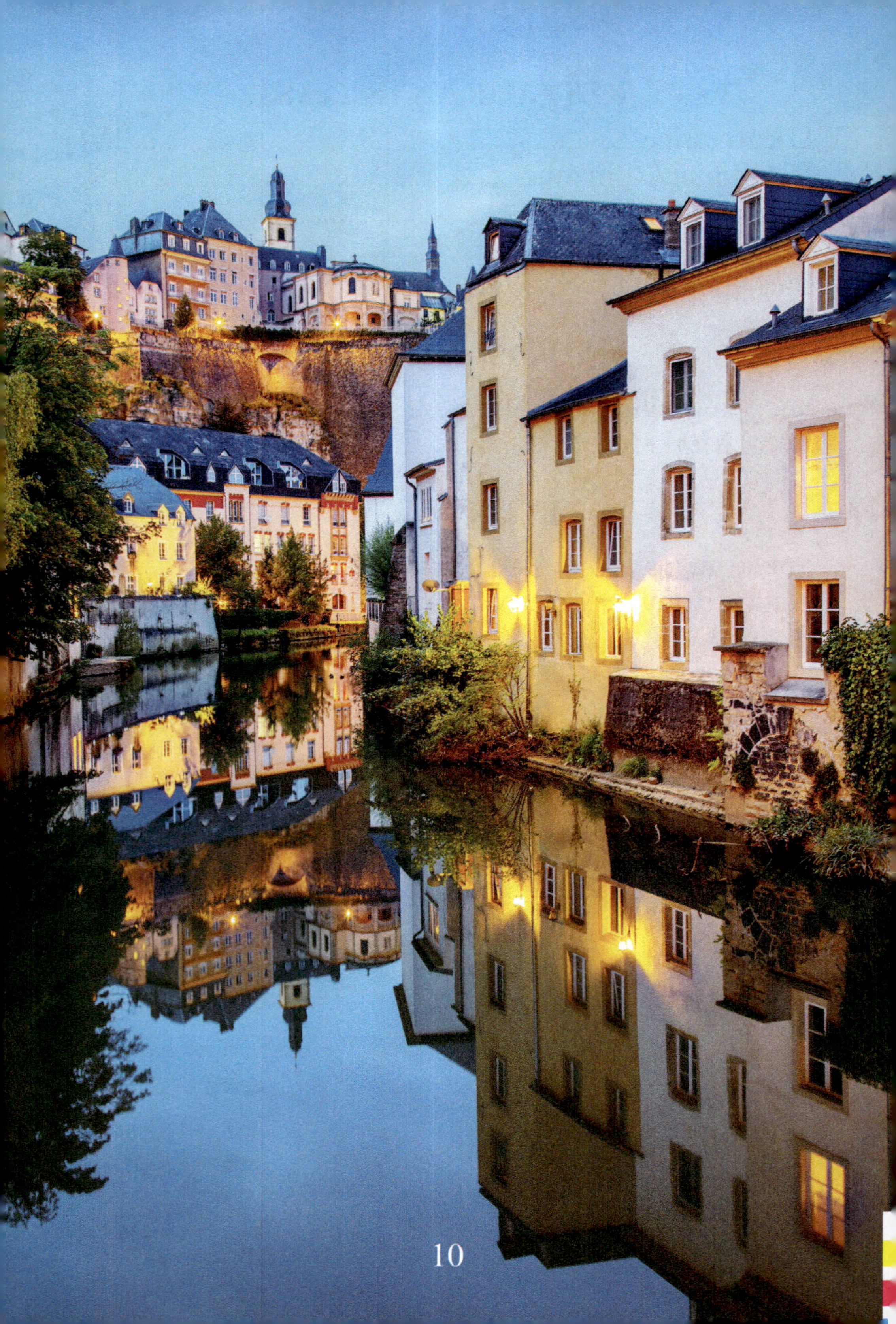

INTRODUCTION

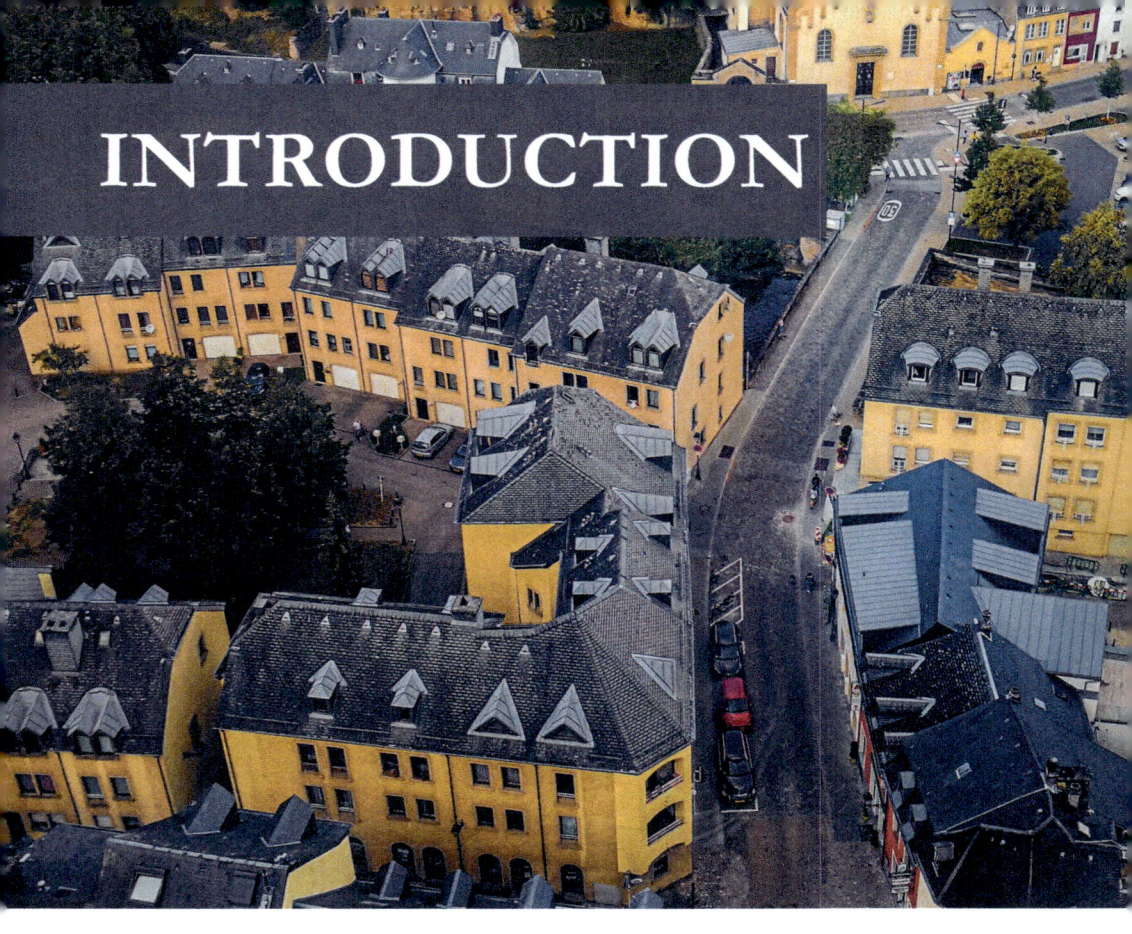

Hey there, outstanding traveller!

First off, a hearty thanks for grabbing this guide. What you've got in your hands is more than mere pages—it's a compass to the wonders of one of the globe's most enthralling destinations.
Now, you might be thinking, "Can't I find all this stuff online, on blogs and travel sites?" Sure, the web is brimming with info, but here's the twist with this guide. It's not just any run-of-the-mill info; it's the real deal. We're serving up insider hints that'll elevate your journey from great to absolutely unforgettable.

What Sets This Guide Apart?

It's not merely text on a page; this guide bursts to life with vivid, full-color photographs that immerse you in Luxembourg's beauty—so you're not just reading; you're witnessing!

Effortlessly Structured
We understand that trip planning can be daunting. That's why we've meticulously organized the guide to make it feel like you're traveling with a savvy companion who knows exactly what you need and when.

Saves Time and Energy
We've done the research for you. With this guide in hand, you've saved countless hours. Now, you can devote more time to experiencing Luxembourg and less to planning.

How To Navigate This Guide

Move at Your Own Speed: Tailor your reading to your interests—dive into the most tantalizing sections first, or take it from the beginning. It's entirely up to you.

Set Realistic Expectations: We aim to provide the latest, top-notch information, but remember, travel is full of surprises. Use this guide as your foundation and embrace the unexpected twists along the way.

Ready for Adventure?
The Luxembourg Travel Guide 2024 isn't just a book; it represents extensive research, authentic encounters, and a deep love for exploration. Cheers to a remarkable trip ahead! Here's to crafting an experience you'll never forget.

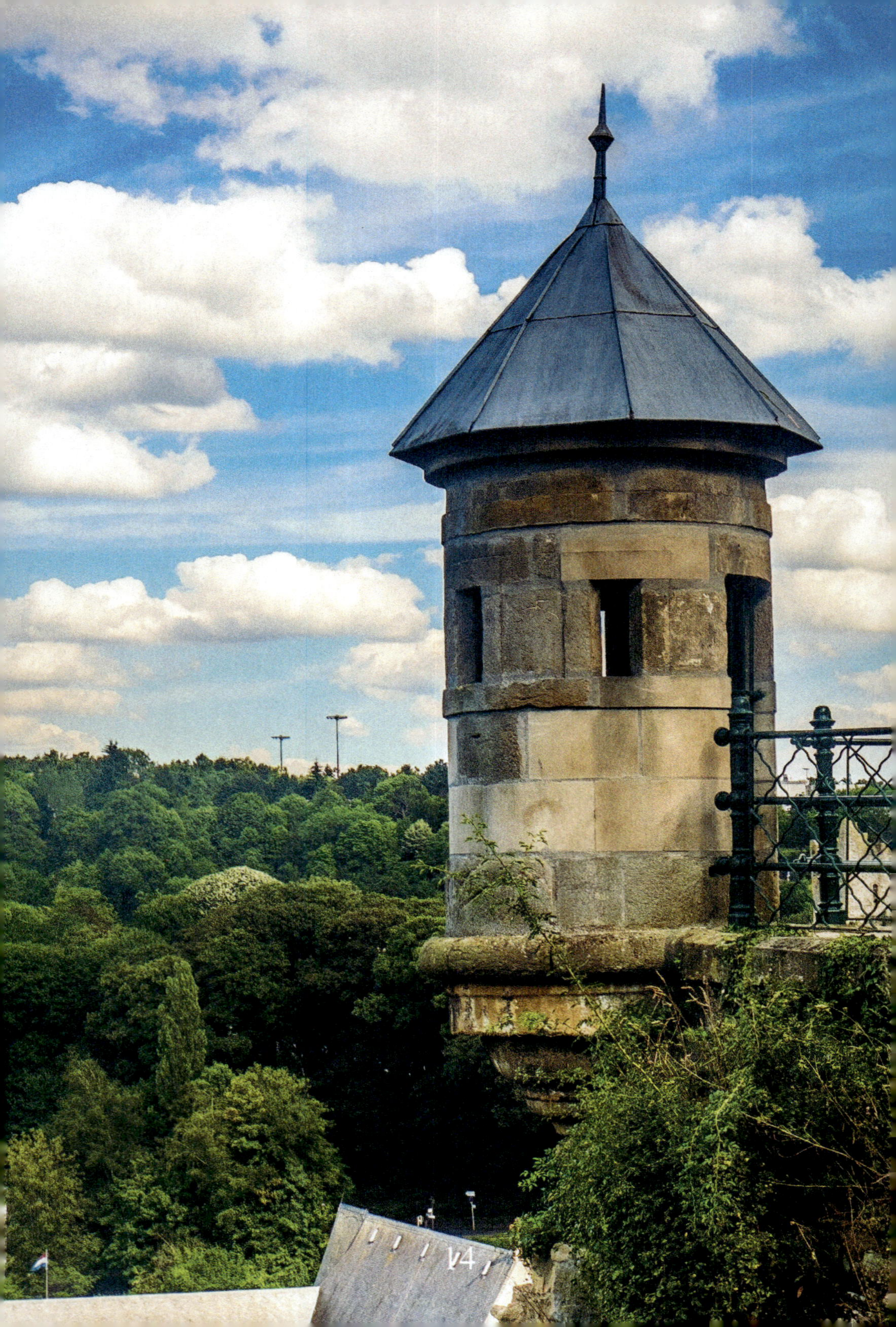

TOP REASONS TO VISIT LUXEMBOURG IN 2024

Rich Culture and History

Free Public Transportation

Stunning Scenery

Wide Range of Dining Options

A Safe and Welcoming Country

Enchanting Towns and Cities

Beautiful Countryside

Convenient Vacation Location

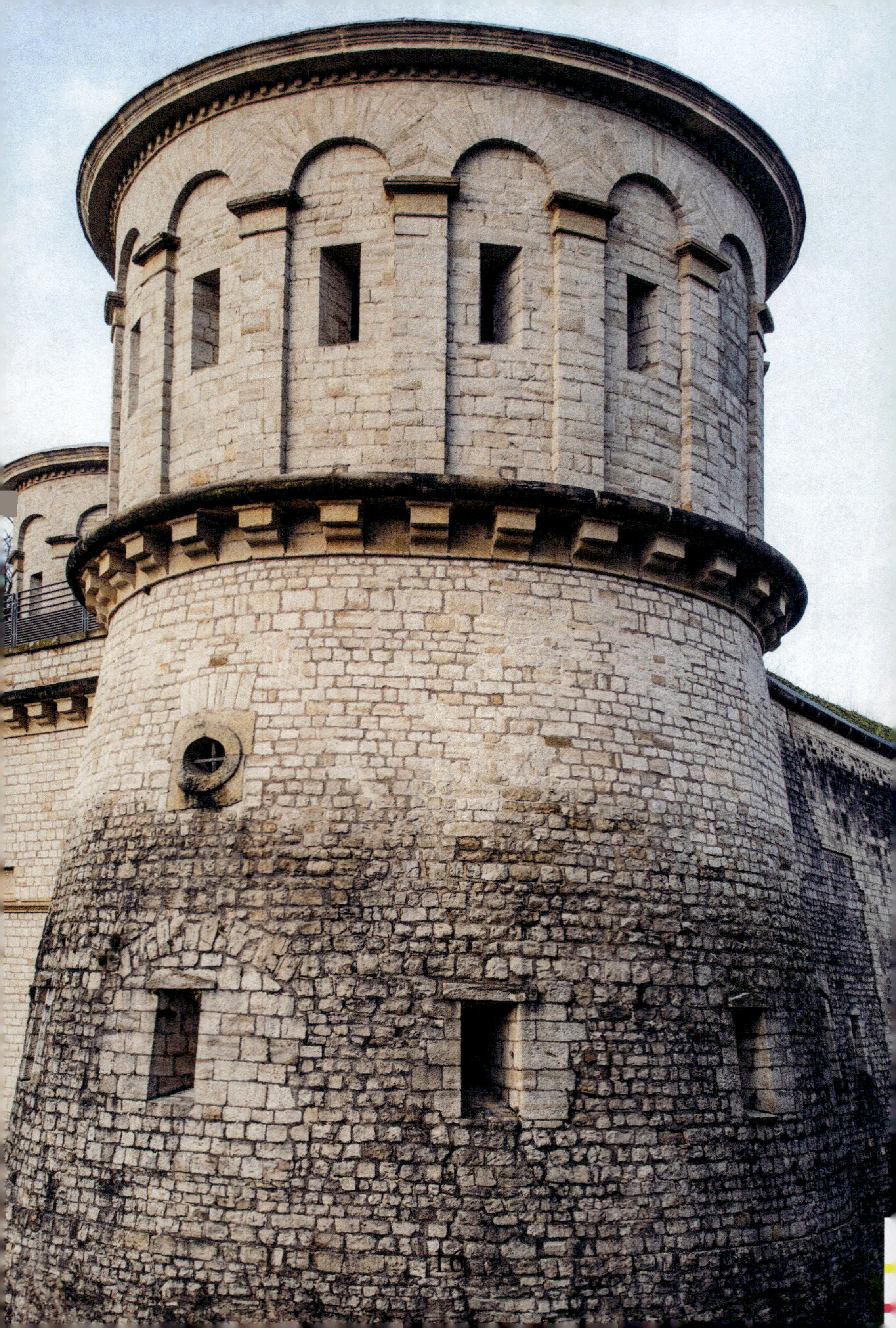

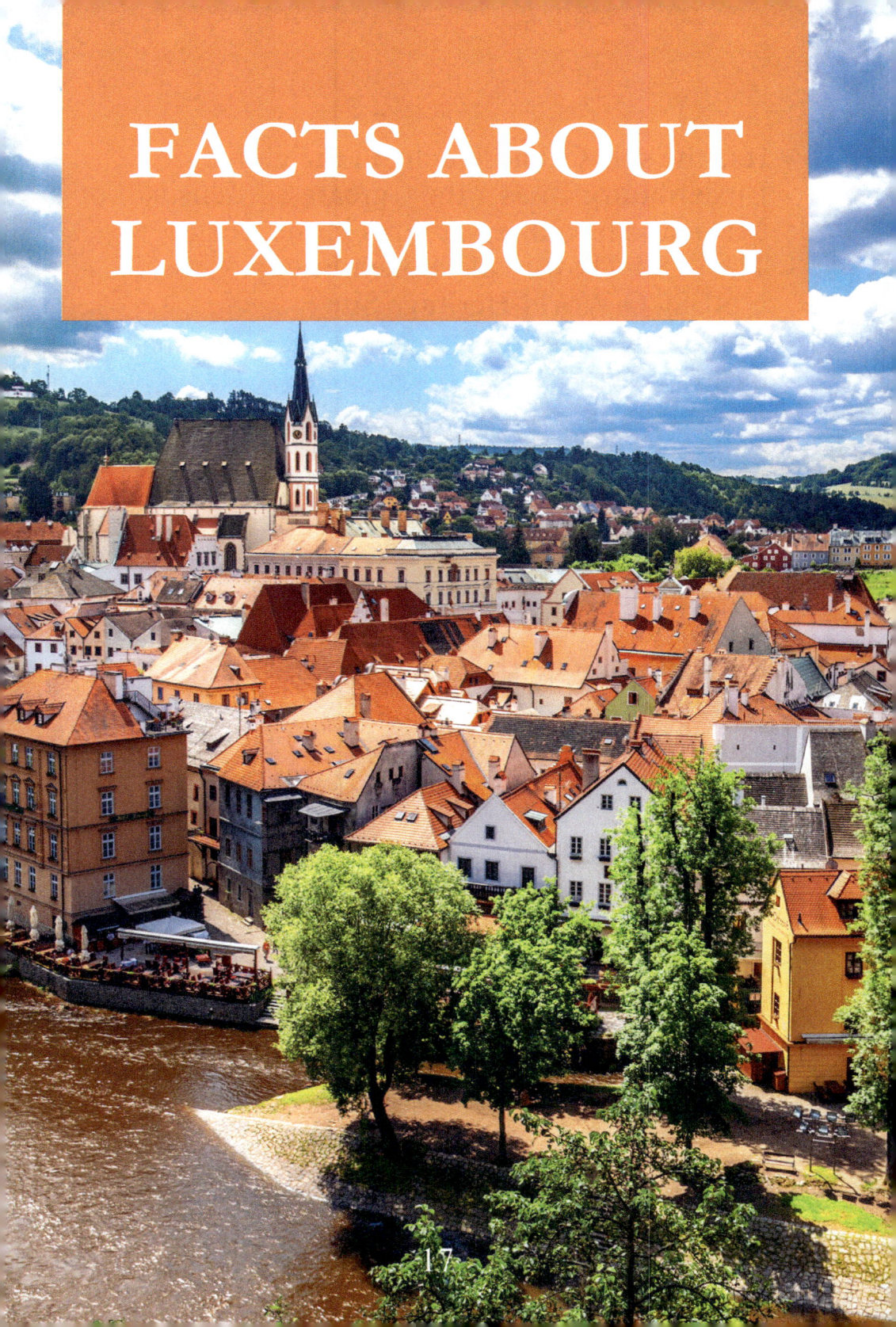

FACTS ABOUT LUXEMBOURG

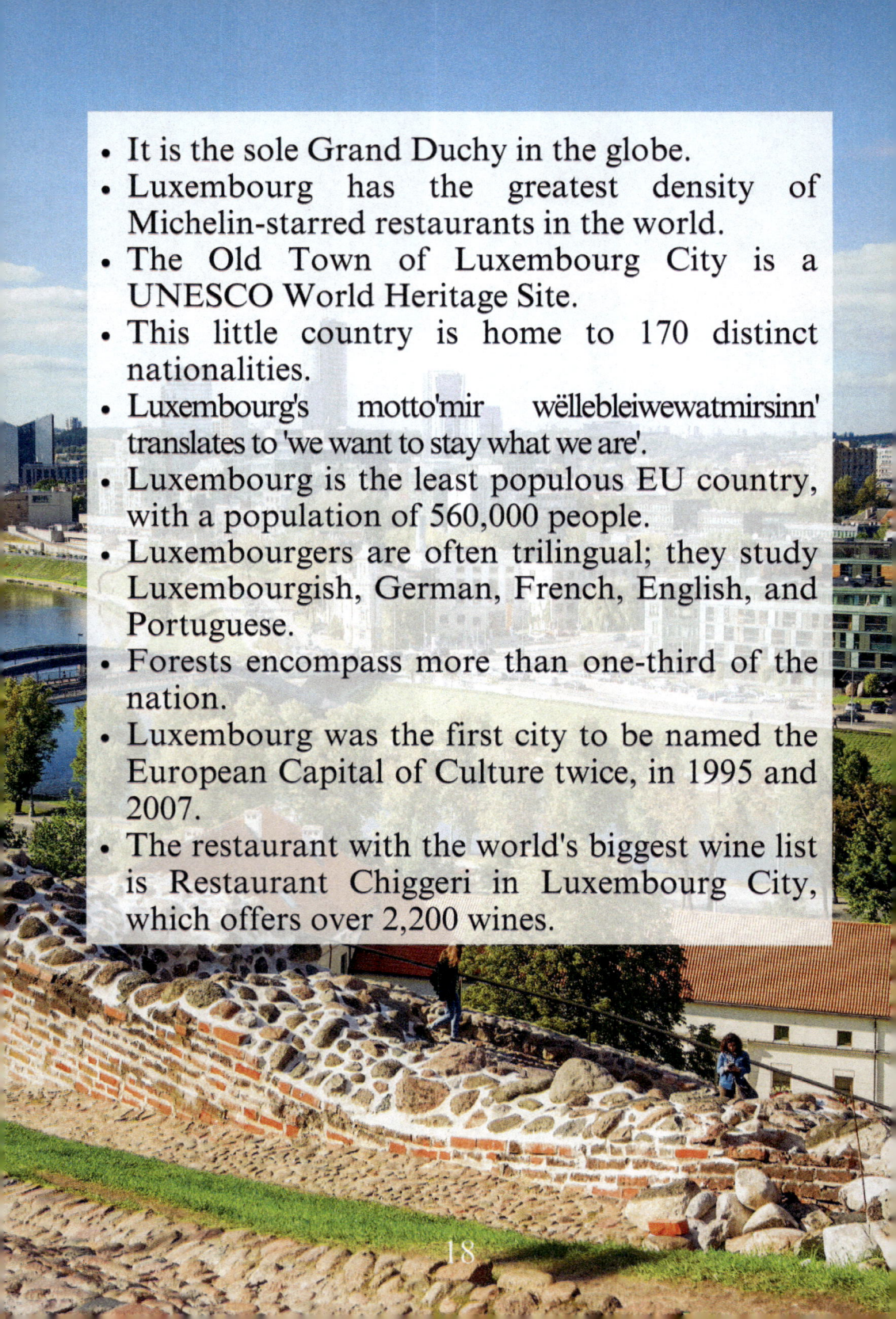

- It is the sole Grand Duchy in the globe.
- Luxembourg has the greatest density of Michelin-starred restaurants in the world.
- The Old Town of Luxembourg City is a UNESCO World Heritage Site.
- This little country is home to 170 distinct nationalities.
- Luxembourg's motto 'mir wëllebleiwewatmirsinn' translates to 'we want to stay what we are'.
- Luxembourg is the least populous EU country, with a population of 560,000 people.
- Luxembourgers are often trilingual; they study Luxembourgish, German, French, English, and Portuguese.
- Forests encompass more than one-third of the nation.
- Luxembourg was the first city to be named the European Capital of Culture twice, in 1995 and 2007.
- The restaurant with the world's biggest wine list is Restaurant Chiggeri in Luxembourg City, which offers over 2,200 wines.

BASIC COMMUNICATION WORDS

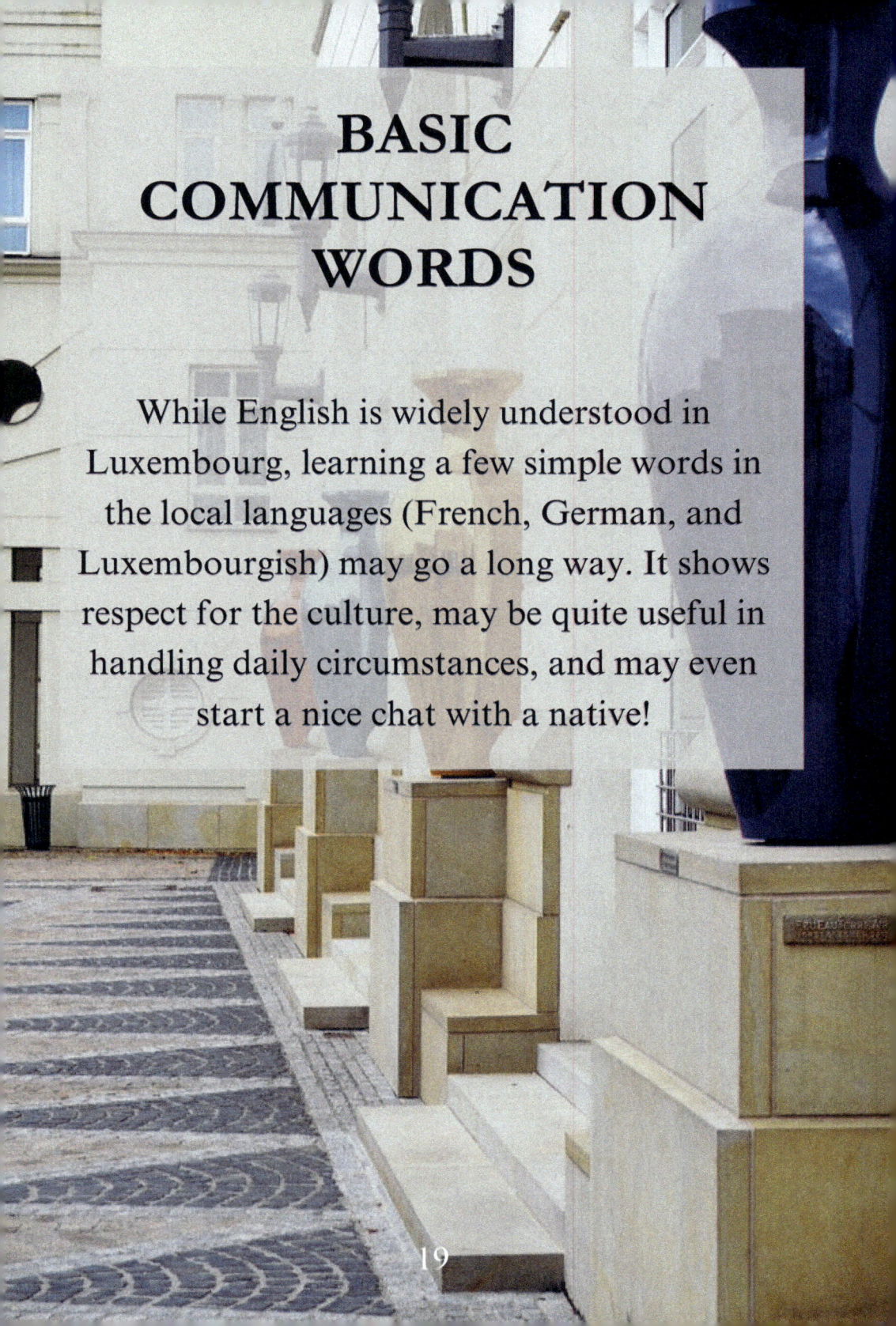

While English is widely understood in Luxembourg, learning a few simple words in the local languages (French, German, and Luxembourgish) may go a long way. It shows respect for the culture, may be quite useful in handling daily circumstances, and may even start a nice chat with a native!

Greetings and Common Courtesy:
- Hello: Moien (pronounced as mwah-yen)
- Goodbye: Äddi (pronounced as eh-dee)
- Thank you: Merci (pronounced as mer-see)
- You're welcome: Gern geschéi (pronounced as gern geh-shy)
- Please: W.e.g. (pronounced as vay eh geh)
- Excuse me: Pardon (pronounced as par-don)
- Yes: Jo (pronounced as yo)
- No: Neen (pronounced as neen)
- Do you speak English?: Sprécht Dir Englesch? (pronounced as shprecht deer eeng-lesh)

Getting Around:
- Where is...?: Wo ass...? (pronounced as vo ahss)
- Can you help me?: Kannst du mir helfen? (pronounced as kanst doo
- meer helfen)
- Can I take a taxi?: Kann ech en Taxi huelen? (pronounced as kan ech en taxee hoo-eln)
- Train station: Gare (pronounced as gahr)
- Bus station: Busbahnhof (pronounced as boos-bahn-hof)

20

- Airport: Fluchhafen (pronounced as fluke-hah-fen)
- Ticket: Ticket (pronounced same as English)
- Left: Lénks (pronounced as lenks)
- Right: Riets (pronounced as reets)
- Straight: Geradeaus (pronounced as geh-rah-deh-owsss)

Numbers (1-10):
- One: Eent (pronounced as aynt)
- Two: Zwee (pronounced as tsvey)
- Three: Dräi (pronounced as dry)
- Four: Véier (pronounced as feer)
- Five: Fënnef (pronounced as fen-nef)
- Six: Séchs (pronounced as zex)
- Seven: Siwen (pronounced as see-ven)
- Eight: Acht (pronounced as ahkt)
- Nine: Néng (pronounced as nang)
- Ten: Zéng (pronounced as tsang)

Essential Phrases:
- How much is this?: Wé vill kascht dat? (pronounced as vay feel kasht dat)
- I would like...: Ech hätt gärn... (pronounced as ech het gairn)
- Do you have...?: Häs du...? (pronounced as hes doo)
- Water: Waasser (pronounced as vah-ser)

- Coffee: Kaffi (pronounced as kah-fee)
- Beer: Béier (pronounced as bair)
- Food: Iessen (pronounced as ee-sen)
- Bathroom: Toilett (pronounced as twah-let)
- Help!: Hëllef! (pronounced as hel-feh)
- **Emergencies:**
- Police: Police (pronounced same as English)
- Hospital: Spidol (pronounced as shpee-dol)
- Pharmacy: Apdikt (pronounced as app-tikt)
- Fire: Feier (pronounced as fai-er)
- Doctor: Dokter (pronounced as dock-ter)
- I am not feeling well: Mir geet et net gutt. (pronounced as meer geht et net gut)

By being acquainted with some fundamental terms and knowing local norms, you may assure a smooth and pleasurable stay in Luxembourg

ABBREVATIONS AND CODES RESTURANT PRICE CODES

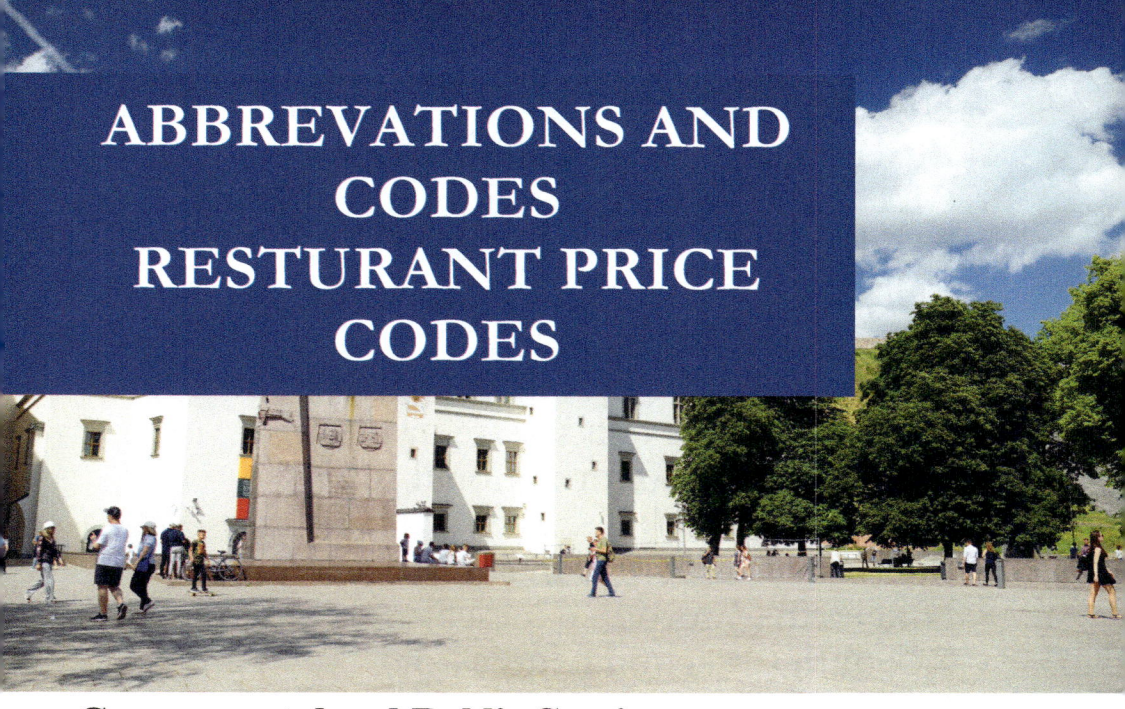

Governmental and Public Services:
- G.-D.: Grand-Ducal (referring to the Grand Duchy of Luxembourg, the official name of the country)
- St.: Saint (used before the name of a saint, e.g., St. Michael's Church)
- Min.: Ministère (Ministry) followed by the specific ministry (e.g., Min. de la Culture - Ministry of Culture)
- Adm.: Administration (used for government departments)
- CFL: Chemins de Fer Luxembourgeois (Luxembourg Railways)
- AVL: Administration des Transports Publics (Public Transportation Administration)
- CLT: Compagnie Luxembourgeoise de Télédiffusion (Luxembourg Broadcasting Company)

23

- UL: Université du Luxembourg (University of Luxembourg)
- CLT-UFA: Centre Luxembourgeois de l'Audiovisuel (Luxembourg Audiovisual Centre)

Locations and Directions:
- Av.: Avenue (used for major roads)
- Pl.: Place (refers to a square or plaza)
- Rte.: Route (used for national roads)
- Cr.: Rue (Street)
- Bd.: Boulevard (wide avenue)
- N.: North (directional indicator)
- S.: South (directional indicator)
- E.: East (directional indicator)
- W.: West (directional indicator)
- C.P.: Code Postal (Postal Code)
- Currency and Taxes:
- €: Euro (the official currency of Luxembourg)
- CHF: Swiss Franc (sometimes accepted in Luxembourg, alongside the Euro)
- TVA: Taxe sur la Valeur Ajoutée (Value Added Tax, typically 17%)

Understanding Prices:
- Prix net: Net price (excluding VAT)
- Prix brut: Gross price (including VAT)

Public Transportation:
- SN CFL: Société Nationale des Chemins de Fer Luxembourgeois (National Company of Luxembourg Railways)
- AVL: Administration des Transports Publics (Public Transportation Administration)

- Gare: Train Station
- Arrêt: Bus Stop

Other Abbreviations:
- a.s.b.l.: Association sans but lucratif (Non-profit organization)
- S.A.: Société Anonyme (Public Limited Company)
- S.à r.l.: Société à responsabilité limitée (Limited Liability Company)
- Tél.: Téléphone (Telephone)
- Fax: Télécopieur (Fax)

RESTURANT PRICE CODES

€ (Single Euro Symbol): This symbol represents the currency used in Luxembourg.

Price Range:
- $ - €€ (Budget-Friendly) Expect lunches to cost between €10 and €20 per person. This category covers cafes, bistros, and ethnic eateries that serve fast nibbles, sandwiches, salads, and affordable local delicacies.
- €€€ - €€€€ (Moderate) This mid-range category includes most eateries, with meals ranging from €20 to €40 per person. There are several different cuisines available, including Italian, French, Luxembourgish, and Asian.
- €€€€€ - €€€€€€ (Fine Dining) Get ready to indulge! This group includes high-end restaurants with an upmarket environment and gourmet cuisine. Expect lunches to cost more than €40 per person, with the sky being the limit for additional activities.

Tips for Savvy Spenders
- Lunch Versus Dinner: Lunch menus are typically less expensive than supper menus, making them an excellent chance to sample local dishes without breaking the budget.
- Daily Specials: During midday, many restaurants offer fixed-price menus ("formule du jour" in French), which provide good value for a multicourse meal.
- Neighborhood jewels: Venture beyond the tourist destinations to find hidden jewels frequented by locals. You may typically find lower costs and a more real environment.
- Embrace the Terrace: During nice weather, choose outside sitting. Many restaurants offer terrace dining at pricing equivalent to indoor seats, allowing you to soak up the local atmosphere.

Additional considerations:
- Drinks: Drinks can greatly increase your cost. Be aware of beverage pricing, particularly for bottled water and alcoholic beverages.
- Tipping: Tipping is not required in Luxembourg, however, a little gratuity (about 10%) is often appreciated for excellent service.

ABOUT LUXEMBOURG

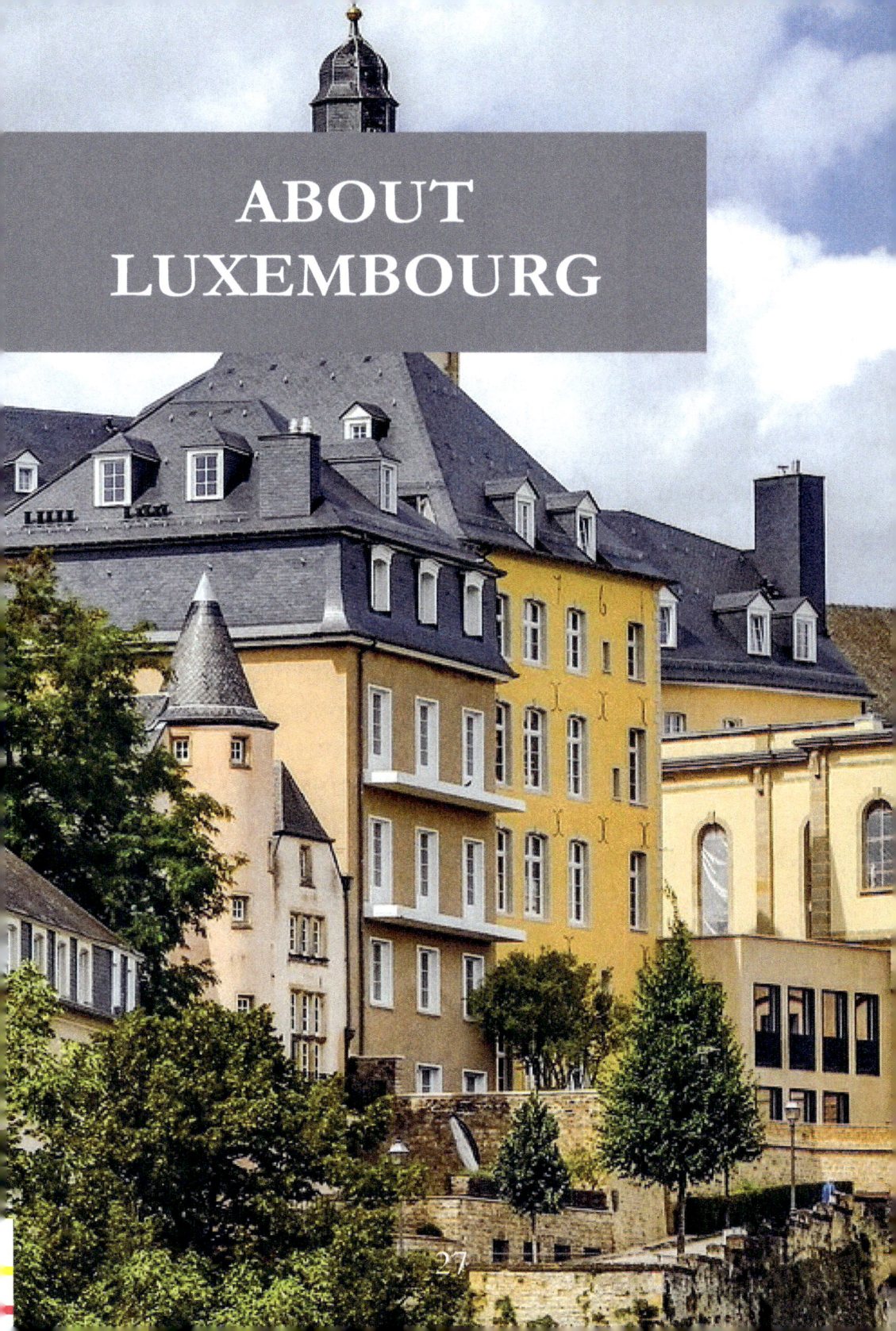

Luxembourg may be a small nation nestled in Europe, cozily bordered by Belgium, France, and Germany, but don't let its size fool you. This country is a tapestry of lush countryside, with the expansive Ardennes forest and natural reserves up north, the craggy ravines of the Mullerthal area to the east, and the charming Moselle river valley down southeast. The capital, Luxembourg City, boasts an iconic ancient fortress that dramatically towers over stark cliffs.

Though it's not the largest of countries, Luxembourg is a treasure trove when it comes to culture, arts, and a rich tapestry of history. It's dotted with enchanting medieval fortresses and renowned wineries. But Luxembourg is more than just a pretty sight; it plays a pivotal role in the European Union today, housing the Court of Justice of the European Communities. Indeed, Luxembourg is a country with its unique flair and a diverse array of offerings.

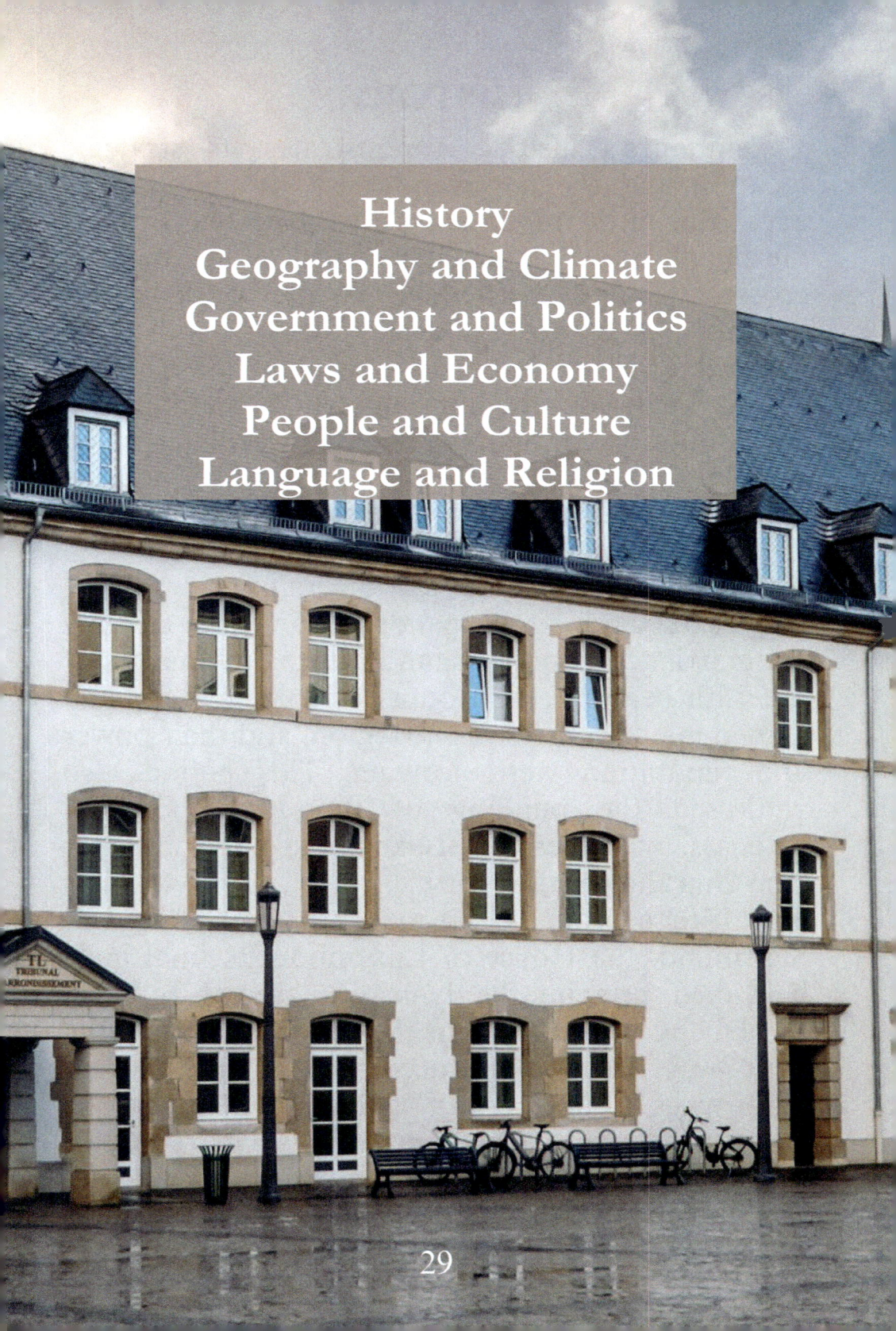

History
Geography and Climate
Government and Politics
Laws and Economy
People and Culture
Language and Religion

HISTORY

Luxembourg's history demonstrates its strategic location and the perseverance of its people. For ages, this little republic nestled between France, Germany, and Belgium has served as an imperial crossroads and battlefield. While evidence of human existence dates back millennia, Luxembourg's written history began in 963 AD.

Count Siegfried, a cunning nobleman, purchased a rocky outcrop containing a Roman fort, later called Lucilinburhuc ("little fortress"). This commemorated the birth of Luxembourg City and the establishment of the House of Luxembourg. The subsequent centuries saw an era of growth.

Siegfried's successors expanded their realm steadily via marriages, conquests, and astute diplomacy. By the 13th century, the Counts of Luxembourg had gained major control of the region, and their power and reputation were growing. This period also witnessed the building of the city's powerful defenses, which earned Luxembourg the moniker "the Gibraltar of the North."

The 14th century was a turning point. Emperor Sigismund, the House of Luxembourg's final male heir, died, bringing the dynasty to an end. In 1477, the Duchy went to Philip the Good of Burgundy, who was eventually succeeded by the strong Habsburgs. Luxembourg got entangled in the Habsburg-Valois Wars, prized for its strategic location. France made many attempts to conquer the Duchy, but the Habsburgs stood fast.

The Eighty Years' War began in the sixteenth century when the Dutch revolted against Spanish Habsburg control. Luxembourg, being part of the Spanish Netherlands, was caught in the crossfire.

The Treaty of the Pyrenees in 1659 resulted in a geographical loss for Luxembourg, with numerous strategic fortifications given to France.

The tides of European politics moved again in the nineteenth century. When Belgium rose against Dutch control in 1830, Luxembourg originally joined the movement. However, the Treaty of London of 1839 carved out a dangerous route for the Duchy.

While granting Luxembourg complete sovereignty, it also formed a personal union with the King of the Netherlands. Belgium also gained control of Luxembourg's primarily French-speaking western region. This loss cemented Luxembourg's identity as a predominantly German-speaking state, albeit French cultural influence remained significant.

The Treaty of London also designated Luxembourg a continuously neutral state, which was guaranteed by the main European powers. This neutrality became critical during the turbulent twentieth century. Despite being violated by Germany throughout both World Wars, Luxembourg's toughness and strategic importance eventually secured its existence.

Following WWII, Luxembourg entered a new period of collaboration. It was a founding member of the Benelux Economic Union and later a prominent participant in the European Coal and Steel Community, which preceded the European Union.

Luxembourg's strategic position, competent workforce, and advantageous tax rules supported a robust financial industry, propelling the country to prominence as an international banking hub.

Today, the Grand Duchy of Luxembourg exists as a tribute to its long and complicated past. A little nation formed in the crucible of European strife, it has become a symbol of solidarity and collaboration.

Luxembourg continues to play an important role in the European Union, with a strong voice despite its small. With a dynamic multicultural culture and a thriving economy, this little nation's future seems promising, a monument to its people's perseverance.

Geography and Climate

Geographically, the Grand Duchy is divided into two sections. The forested and hilly northern half of the country is a continuation of the Belgian Ardennes.

In the south, the Lorraine Plateau extends from France, creating an open, rolling countryside with an average elevation of 1,000 feet. The Our, Sure, and Moselle Rivers flow north-south along the frontier between Luxembourg and Germany.

OUR RIVER

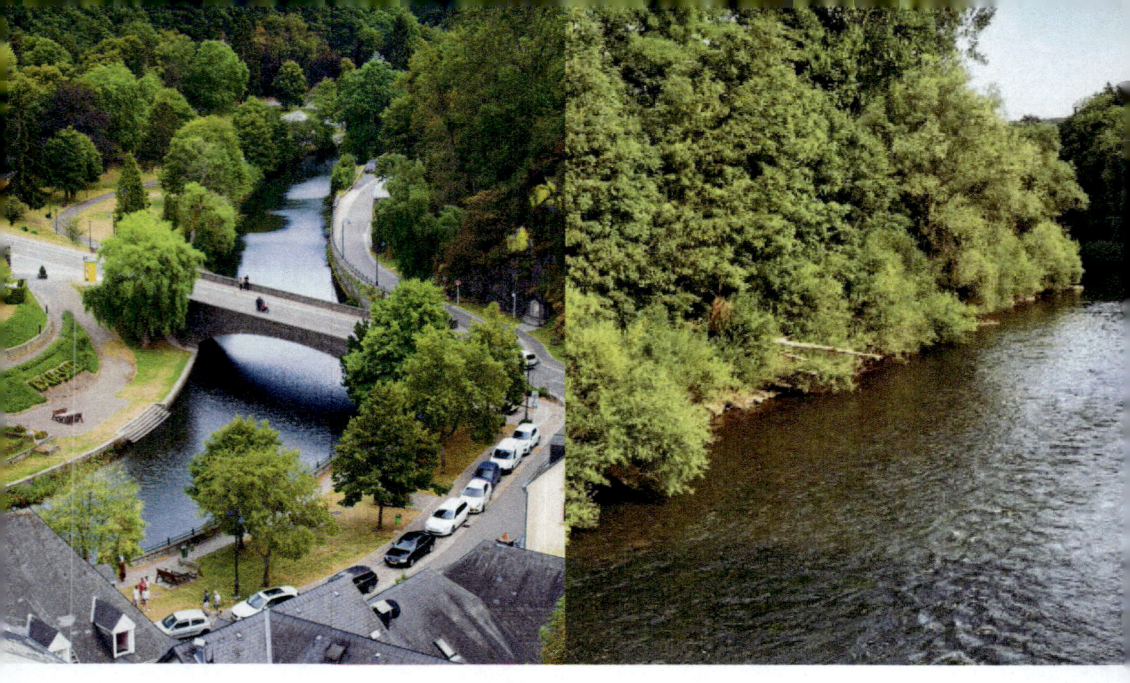

SURE RIVER

MOSELLE RIVER

Geographic Location	Europe
Total Area	998 Square Miles 2,586 Square Kilometers
Land Area	998 Square Miles 2,586 Square Kilometers
Land Boundaries	223 Miles 359 Kilometers
Border Countries	Belgium 148 km, France 73 km, Germany 138 km
Geographic Coordinates	49 45 N, 6 10 E
Terrain	mostly gently rolling uplands with broad, shallow valleys; uplands to slightly mountainous in the north; steep slope down to Moselle flood plain in the southeast
Highest Point	559 Meters
Highest Point Location	Buurgplaatz 559 m
Lowest Point	133 Meters
Lowest Point Location	Moselle River 133 m
Natural Resources	iron ore (no longer exploited), arable land
Time Zone	UTC+1 (6 hours ahead of Washington, DC, during Standard Time)

Government and Politics

The head of state is a hereditary role held by the Grand Duke, presently Henri. But much of his power is ceremonial. Regardless of the outcome of the elections, he selects the Prime Minister but has little executive power.

Luxembourg is a constitutional monarchy with a parliamentary democracy underpinning its operations. The people own sovereignty, and they wield it via their duly chosen representatives in the Chamber of Deputies, often known as the Parliament.

Every five years, voters above the age of eighteen are required to cast ballots to choose the sixty members of the A wide variety of political parties are guaranteed a voice thanks to proportional representation.

A majority is rarely held by one party. Parties form coalitions following elections, with the head of the largest party serving as prime minister. For example, the Democratic Party (DP), the Luxembourg Socialist Workers' Party (LSAP), and the Green Party (DG) form the coalition that governs the country currently.

The prime minister is in charge of the Council of Government, or cabinet, which is made up of several ministers in charge of different ministries. They are in charge of enacting and carrying out laws as the executive branch.

The Grand Duke still has some authority even if his position is ceremonial. In extraordinary situations, he has the authority to dissolve the parliament and oversee the creation of the government.

The court serves as a stand-alone check on the legislative and executive branches. Because judges are appointed for life, judicial processes are guaranteed to be unbiased.

There are several parties in Luxembourg's multiparty system, each of which represents a distinct ideology. Although the Christian Social People's Party (CSV) has always held a majority, the DP, LSAP, and Greens have gained ground in the most recent elections.

Laws

The legal system of Luxembourg is deeply rooted in the ideas of civil law. As a result, laws are codified and heavily rely on written legislation and established court precedents. For both locals and guests, this strategy provides consistency and predictability.

Luxembourg's legal system is closely entwined with EU law because it was a founding member of the EU. A feeling of familiarity is ensured by the bloc's many unified rules and regulations, especially for tourists from Europe. Furthermore, this integration ensures respect for basic freedoms and human rights—two essential European ideals.

Crucial Rules for Travelers:
- General Laws: Luxembourg complies with the fundamental rights stated in the European Convention on Human Rights. This implies that you should anticipate legislation safeguarding your freedom of speech, privacy, and safety.
- Currency: The Euro is still the accepted form of payment. When planning your travel budget, take currency rates into account.
- Permits and Visas: Depending on your country of residence and length of stay, different criteria apply for visas. Visit the website of Luxembourg's Ministry of Foreign and European Affairs to get the most recent information. (https://maee.gouvernement.lu/).

- Traffic Laws: Drive on the right side of the road. Speed limits are strictly enforced to preserve road safety.
- Safety and Security: Luxembourg has a very low crime rate. However, remaining attentive, particularly in congested locations, is always advisable.

Specific Legal Considerations:
- Data Protection: Luxembourg closely enforces the EU's General Data Protection Regulation (GDPR). Businesses and organizations must follow severe laws for data collection, storage, and utilization. This leads to robust data privacy safeguards for visitors.
- Consumer Rights: Luxembourgish legislation guarantees robust consumer protection rights. You are entitled to information, fair contracts, and remedies in the event of a disagreement with a firm.
- Alcohol and Drugs: Luxembourg's legal drinking age is 18. Drug regulations are rather severe, with punishments varied according to the type and quantity of the substance.

Recent Developments and Trends
- Luxembourg is actively integrating sustainability ideas into its legislative system. During your stay, you may come across rules that promote environmental preservation and good corporate practices.

- Evolving Labor Laws: The government is continually evaluating and amending labor laws to suit the changing work environment. This might include legislation regarding the minimum wage, worker rights, and remote employment options.

Important Resources:
- Ministry of Justice (French): https://justice.public.lu/
- Luxembourg National Institute of Statistics and Economic Studies (STATEC) (French & English): https://statistiques.public.lu/

Laws may be subject to change. It's always a good idea to check for updates around your travel date.

Economy

Steel is the foundation of Luxembourg's economy. For decades, the steel sector served as the foundation of the nation's economy. While its importance has lessened, steel manufacturing remains important, and Luxembourgish steel is well-known for its quality.

Luxembourg's growth as a financial hub demonstrates its strategic wisdom. Taking advantage of its political stability and favorable rules, the country rose to the top of the global asset management, investment banking, and private wealth management rankings. While the environment is changing, Luxembourg remains a major participant in the financial world.

Recognizing the constraints of over-reliance on a single industry, Luxembourg has aggressively explored diversification. Logistics and information and communication technologies (ICT) are increasingly significant contributions, with the country developing as a European leader in logistics hubs. Exciting developments are also underway in the space industry, with Luxembourg promoting itself as a center for space exploration and commercial operations.

Luxembourg's unique location at the crossroads of major European economies has contributed significantly to its prosperity. The country has a very open economy, with exports surpassing its GDP. This openness promotes innovation and economic progress by allowing for easier access to international markets.

While openness has many benefits, it also increases reliance on foreign economic partners. Global economic fluctuations and disruptions to international trade can have a significant impact on Luxembourg's economy.

The value of the Euro relative to your native currency may affect your purchasing power. Budgeting apps or cost-tracking tools may be handy.

Luxembourg has a strong economy, which translates into a decent standard of living. Expect to witness well-maintained infrastructure, efficient public services, and a focus on quality throughout your journey.

Luxembourg is increasingly integrating sustainability principles into its economic structure. During your journey, you may come across initiatives that promote environmental preservation and ethical business practices, demonstrating the country's commitment to a greener future.

The government actively encourages innovation through initiatives like the Fit for Future program, which sponsors research and development in a range of fields. Luxembourg's concentration on innovation positions it for future economic growth and leadership in new markets.

Luxembourg quickly recovered from the COVID-19 epidemic, but the situation in Ukraine has created new challenges. To ensure long-term economic stability, the government is addressing inflationary pressures and labor shortages.

People and Culture

The Luxembourgish people, who make up nearly half of the population, are the heart of the nation. Their language, Letzebuergesch, a mix of Germanic dialects and French influences, is a treasured emblem of their own identity.

Luxembourg has a rich multicultural tapestry. Immigrants from surrounding countries including France, Germany, Belgium, and Portugal, as well as a burgeoning international population, help to shape the country's dynamic cultural landscape.

Multilingualism is a distinguishing feature of Luxembourgish society. The majority of Luxembourgers speak Luxembourgish, French, and German fluently, with English becoming more prevalent. The capacity to speak in several languages symbolizes the country's openness and function as a cultural bridge.

Luxembourg is filled with bright celebrations throughout the year. Carnival, with its brightly colored costumes and parades, is a highlight. Christmas markets, rooted in tradition and featuring delectable local goodies, provide a great winter experience.

The Schueberfouer, a centuries-old funfair hosted yearly in Luxembourg City, is a renowned event that includes amusement rides, wonderful food vendors, and a celebratory atmosphere.

Folklore plays an important role in Luxembourgish culture. From traditional dances like the

"Sprangprozession" to local crafts and storytelling traditions, you'll see glimpses of the country's rich legacy as you explore.

Luxembourgish cuisine is a lovely fusion of French and German traditions, with substantial comfort foods taking center stage. Local popular dishes include "Judd mat Gaardebounen" (smoked neck with broad beans) and "Bouchée à la Reine" (a puff pastry filled with ragù).

Luxembourg's culinary landscape is not restricted to traditional dishes. The country has an increasing number of Michelin-starred restaurants that serve unique and contemporary food.

Luxembourgish wine. The Moselle Valley produces world-class Riesling and Pinot Gris grapes. For those looking for alternatives, local brews and strong coffee are popular options.

Luxembourgers are noted for their courteousness and regard for others. While initially hesitant, they are truly open to tourists who are interested in their culture and customs.

A strong feeling of community is an important element in Luxembourgish society. Local festivals and gatherings frequently have a sociable and welcoming environment, which fosters a sense of belonging.

Luxembourg embraces a unique blend of tradition and modernity. While holding onto their heritage, Luxembourgish people are also forward-thinking and technologically savvy.

Language and Religion

Letzebuergesch, or Luxembourgish, is central to the country's linguistic identity. This intriguing language, spoken by about half of the population, is a West Central German dialect greatly affected by French and other Germanic languages. Luxembourg's cultural scene is enriched by its peculiar language and amusing sounds.

Multilingualism is a distinguishing feature of Luxembourgish society. Historically, the country acted as a hub for trade and cultural interchange, encouraging the spread of numerous languages. The majority of Luxembourgers speak Luxembourgish, French, and German fluently, with English becoming more prevalent. The capacity to speak in several languages symbolizes the country's openness and function as a cultural bridge.

As the official languages of the country, French, German, and Letzebuergesch are all equal. This trilingualism is visible in official papers, public signs, and the educational system. Understanding these three languages enables easy movement inside Luxembourgish society.

Letzebuergesch's route to becoming a national treasure was not always straightforward. For generations, it was seen as a simple vernacular, sometimes eclipsed by French and German. However, in the twentieth century, a national identity movement resulted in the formal acknowledgment of Letzebuergesch and an increase in national pride linked with the language.

Letzebuergesch is currently being standardized and promoted for use in all aspects of everyday life. A national language institute regulates spelling and grammar, and educational initiatives aim to ensure the language's survival for future generations.

Roman Catholicism has historically been the dominant religion in Luxembourg. For centuries, the Catholic Church was instrumental in shaping the country's social and cultural landscape. Even today, Catholicism remains the religion of choice for a sizable proportion of the population.

Luxembourg's religious landscape is being transformed. Immigration and secularization have led to an increase in religious diversity. Protestantism, Judaism, and Islam are all represented in the country, and an increasing number of people identify as non-religious.

Luxembourg is committed to religious freedom and tolerance. This enables the peaceful coexistence of different faiths, fostering a sense of inclusivity and respect for individual beliefs.

PRATICAL INFORMATION

Visa Requirements and Documents
Currency and Rate of Exchange
Cultural etiquette
International Telephone and useful Telephone Numbers
Travel Costs to Luxembourg estimated in Budget-friendly, Mid range and Luxury
Time and Electricity
Transportation Options To and Within Luxembourg
International Flights and Major Airports

Visa Requirements and Documents

The first step is to determine whether you need a visa to enter Luxembourg. This depends on your nationality and the length of your anticipated stay.
- Visa-free Entry: Citizens of the European Union (EU), European Economic Area (EEA), and Switzerland can enter Luxembourg without a visa for stays of up to 90 days during a 180-day period. Only a valid passport is necessary.
- Visa Required: Most citizens of other nations will require a visa to enter Luxembourg. The sort of visa you need depends on the reason for your visit.

The most common visa categories are:
- Tourist visas are for short-term visits for tourist purposes.
- Business Visa: Used for business meetings, conferences, and trade fairs.
- Transit Visa: For tourists traveling through Luxembourg on their way to another destination.

Where to apply:
Visa applications are normally sent to the Luxembourg embassy or consulate in your native country. If there is no Luxembourgish representation in your country, you may need to apply through an embassy or consulate in another Schengen Area nation that represents Luxembourg's interests.

Essential Documents:

Here is a list of documents that are often necessary for a visa application to Luxembourg (exact criteria may vary based on your country and visa category).

- Valid passport: Your passport must be valid for at least three months after your anticipated departure date from Luxembourg, with at least two blank pages for visa stamps.
- Completed Visa Application Form: The application form is available for download on the Luxembourgish Ministry of Foreign and European Affairs' website or via the embassy or consulate.
- Passport-sized photographs: Two current passport-sized pictures that match the Schengen Area criteria.
- Proof of Travel and lodging: A round-trip flight itinerary or booking confirmation, as well as proof of booked lodging for your stay in Luxembourg.
- Travel Medical Insurance: Proof of valid travel medical insurance with at least €30,000 in coverage for medical bills and hospitalization in the event of an emergency.
- Proof of Subsistence: Documents indicating that you have enough money to maintain yourself throughout your stay in Luxembourg. This might include bank statements, evidence of work, or a sponsor's letter of support.

Additional Documents (Depending on Visa Type): Depending on the visa category, extra papers may be required, such as a company invitation letter for a business visa or a letter of invitation from a Luxembourg host for a private visit.

Fees and Processing Time:
There is a non-refundable processing cost associated with visa applications. The charge varies according to the visa category and your nationality. Processing periods might range from a few days to many weeks. It is best to submit your application well in advance of your anticipated travel date.

Additional Considerations:
- Biometric data collection During the application process, you may need to provide your fingerprints and a digital image. This is routine practice for Schengen visas.
- Many Entry Visas: If you want to visit Luxembourg on many occasions in a short period, you might consider applying for a multiple-entry visa rather than a single-entry visa.
- Visa Extension: Extending your stay in Luxembourg may require asking for a visa extension within the country. For more information, consult with the appropriate authorities.

Important Resources:
- Ministry of Foreign and European Affairs of Luxembourg: https://maee.gouvernement.lu/ (French & English)

- VisaGuide.World: Luxembourg Visa Requirements
https://visaguide.world/europe/luxembourg-visa/

Currency and Rate of Exchange

Luxembourg, has used the Euro as its official currency since 1999. This means you won't come across a different Luxembourgian currency and may spend Euros across the country.

However, if your home currency is not the Euro, you must consider conversion rates to ensure a seamless financial experience throughout your vacation.

The Euro's exchange rate varies every day versus other currencies.

There are various options for exchanging your cash for Euros before or during your trip:
- Your local bank: This can be a convenient alternative, but the prices may not be the most competitive.
- Currency Exchange Bureaus: These provide a quick and straightforward way to exchange currencies, but the costs might be expensive.
- ATMs in Luxembourg: Withdrawing Euros from ATMs with your debit or credit card is a popular choice. Be mindful of any ATM fees and international transaction costs imposed by your bank.
- Travel Cards: Prepaid travel cards filled with Euros can be a secure and handy method to handle your money while traveling.

Here are some resources to check the current exchange rate: **European Central Bank , XE Currency Converter**

Cultural etiquette

Understanding Luxembourgish cultural etiquette can help you interact with the people smoothly and courteously while on your vacation.

Here's a complete guide on navigating the social practices and traditions that make up Luxembourgish society:

Greetings and Introductions:

Firm Handshake: The handshake is the most usual way to welcome in Luxembourg. A solid handshake with direct eye contact indicates confidence and respect.

Formal Greetings: When greeting someone for the first time, use titles such as "Monsieur" (Mr.) or "Madame" (Ms.), followed by their surname. Titles such as "Herr" (Mr.) and "Frau" (Ms.) are also understood, indicating a German influence. Younger generations may utilize their first names after a first introduction.

Hello in Letzebuergesch: A simple "Moien" (pronounced "moy-en") is a flexible greeting that may be used at any time of day, much like "Hello" or "Good morning/afternoon."

Dining Etiquette

Punctuality is Valued: Aim to appear on time for dinner invites. For formal occasions, dress modestly but smartly, whereas for informal meetings should be dressed a little more informally.

Table Manners: Continental European table manners are commonly observed. When not eating, keep your hands in your lap, use proper utensils, and avoid chatting with your mouth full.

Wine Etiquette: The host usually starts the toast. It is customary to establish eye contact and utter "Santé" (pronounced "sawn-tay") while clinking glasses.

Sharing the cost: Unless specifically indicated differently, the host normally handles the cost. However, asking to pay or divide the cost is a generous gesture.

Social interactions:

Luxembourgish society places a higher priority on personal space than in other countries. Keep a comfortable distance during chats.

Safe discussion subjects include Luxembourg's culture, history, and stunning scenery. Avoid extremely personal or contentious topics.

Public Displays of Affection: In general, public displays of affection are more guarded than in other cultures.

Smoking is not allowed in most public indoor locations, including restaurants and bars. Designated smoking locations are frequently accessible outside.

Gifts and Tips

Bringing a little gift, such as flowers, chocolates, or local wine, to a dinner invitation is a considerate gesture.

Tipping is not required in Luxembourg, however, a little gratuity (between 5 and 10%) is appreciated for good service at restaurants. Tipping taxi drivers is not customary, however, rounding up the fee is standard practice.

Additional Tips

- Dress modestly when visiting religious sites.
- Be mindful of noise levels in public places.
- Queueing is expected in most situations.
- Separate waste disposal is encouraged. Look for designated bins.

International Telephone and useful Telephone Numbers

International Dialing to Luxembourg:
Country Code: To call Luxembourg from overseas, dial +352 followed by the local phone number.
No Trunk Prefix: Unlike some other nations, Luxembourg has a closed dialing system. This implies no extra prefix is required to call between landlines inside the nation. So, if you are already in Luxembourg and want to contact a local number, simply dial the eight-digit phone number.

Useful Phone Numbers:
Here are some important phone numbers to have ready during your vacation to Luxembourg:
- Emergency Services: 112 (This is the one number for emergencies such as fire, police, and ambulance services).
- Police: 113 (non-emergency circumstances).
- Fire Department: 112 (for fire emergency).
- Medical Emergency: 112 (for ambulance services)
- Call (+352) 42 82 82 for general information on Luxembourg.
- Tourist Information: +352 42 82 81 (This number gives tourist information about Luxembourg).

Additional Tips:
Most mobile phone networks provide roaming services in Luxembourg. However, before you travel, check with your mobile operator about roaming rates. Consider getting a local SIM card to get cheaper calling rates.
Public phones are becoming less widespread, but you may still see them at airports, train stations, and public

spaces. These phones usually require phone cards, which may be obtained at newsstands or convenience stores.

Many mobile network operators provide Wi-Fi calling services. This enables you to make calls via a Wi-Fi network, which is a cost-effective choice if you have a restricted data plan.

Travel Costs to Luxembourg

Budget-Friendly Cost Estimated

Average Daily Cost Per person, per day	€ 79
Accommodation Hotel or hostel for one person	€ 39
Local Transportation, Taxis, local buses, subway, etc.	€ 5.21
Intercity Transportation	€ 21
Food, Meals for one day	€ 35
Entertainment Entrance tickets, shows, etc.	€ 4.69
Scams, Robberies, and Mishaps	€ 44
Alcohol, Drinks for one day	€ 4.85

Mid-Range Estimated Cost

Average Daily Cost Per person, per day	€ 184
Accommodation Hotel or hostel for one person	€ 89
Local Transportation, Taxis, local buses, subway, etc.	€ 13
Intercity Transportation	€ 54
Food, Meals for one day	€ 80
Entertainment Entrance tickets, shows, etc.	€ 11
Scams, Robberies, and Mishaps	€ 44
Alcohol, Drinks for one day	€ 11

Luxury Estimated Cost

Average Daily Cost Per person, per day	€ 366
Accommodation Hotel or hostel for one person	€ 173
Local Transportation, Taxis, local buses, subway, etc.	€ 29
Intercity Transportation	€ 139
Food, Meals for one day	€ 159
Entertainment Entrance tickets, shows, etc.	€ 21
Scams, Robberies, and Mishaps	€ 44
Alcohol, Drinks for one day	€ 22

Time and Electricity

Time Zone:
Luxembourg uses Central European Time (CET) throughout the year. This means it is one hour ahead of Coordinated Universal Time (UTC) during normal time and two hours ahead during Daylight Saving Time (DST).
Daylight Saving Time (DST) is observed in Luxembourg, as well as throughout Europe. Clocks are adjusted one hour forward on the last Sunday of March and one hour back on the last Sunday of October.
Align Your Schedule, To avoid any time misunderstanding during your journey, consider these suggestions:
- Adjusting Your Watch: Once you are in Luxembourg, set your watch to Central European Time.
- Online Time Converters: Use online time converters to effortlessly compare Luxembourg time to your native time zone.
- Planning Activities: Consider the time difference while arranging your trip and scheduling activities.

Understanding Luxembourgian Electricity:
- Luxembourg is connected to the European electrical system, ensuring a consistent power supply.
- Voltage and Frequency: In Luxembourg, the standard voltage is 230 volts AC (alternating current) with a frequency of 50 Hertz (Hz). This is consistent throughout most European nations.

- Luxembourg's most frequent plug types are the two-pronged European connector (CEE 7/5) and the three-pronged Schuko plug (CEE 7/7).

Prepare Your Electronics:

To guarantee your electrical equipment perform effectively in Luxembourg, consider the following factors:
- Voltage Compatibility: Check your electrical gadgets' voltage rating (typically located on a label or power adaptor). If your gadget runs on a different voltage (for example, 110 volts in the United States), you'll need a voltage converter to prevent harm.
- Plug Adapters: If your device's plug does not meet Luxembourg's requirements, you will need a travel adapter. These adapters may be purchased online, at electrical stores, or your destination airport.
- Consider a universal travel adapter that can accept a variety of plug types for future trips.

Additional Tips:
- Invest in a surge protector. A surge protector protects your electrical equipment from unexpected power fluctuations.
- Bring a spare battery pack: A portable battery pack can help you keep your gadgets charged while on the road.
- Check with Your Hotel: Many hotels provide universal adapters or make them accessible for purchase.

Transportation Options To and Within Luxembourg

Airport Info:
Address: 4, Rue de Treves B.P. 273 L-2016
Location: Luxembourg Airport is located 8km (5 miles) east of luxembourg city centre
Telephone: +352 24640

Luxembourg Airport (Findel - LUX) is the country's major international airport, conveniently located just east of Luxembourg City. Several major airlines fly from major European cities and beyond, giving it an easy starting point for your trip.

Connecting Flights: For those traveling from farther afield, connecting flights via bigger European airports such as Frankfurt, Paris, or Amsterdam may be essential. Investigate alternatives and maybe lower rates on certain routes.

When you arrive at Findel Airport, you will have various alternatives for getting to your final destination:
- Taxis: Reliable taxi services are generally available, providing a handy, if more expensive, option for getting to your hotel or lodgings.
- Shuttle Bus: A specialized airport shuttle bus connects Findel Airport to Luxembourg City, giving a low-cost and efficient method to get to the center of the activity.
- Luxembourg's well-developed public transportation system includes the airport. Trains and buses link Findel to a variety of places around the country, providing for a smooth transition from air to land travel.

Exploring via train:
- CFL: Your Trusted Rail Companion Chemins de Fer Luxembourgeois (CFL) runs Luxembourg's efficient and large railway network. Trains connect the country's major cities and towns, providing a pleasant, picturesque, and environmentally beneficial mode of transportation.
- CFL trains are known for their timeliness and dependability, ensuring that you get to your destination on time. Relax and enjoy the passing beauty as you travel through Luxembourg's gorgeous landscapes.

- High-Speed Options: For those looking for a speedier connection, the TGV (Train à Grande Vitesse) line runs from Luxembourg City to Paris in slightly over two hours. This allows for day visits to the City of Lights and quick connections to other important French locations.
- Since March 2020, all public transportation in Luxembourg, including trains, has been free to passengers. This wonderful effort makes traveling across the country by rail a very cost-effective and appealing choice.

Exploring via buses

- Extensive Network: Beyond large towns, a substantial bus network run by numerous firms connects even tiny villages and rural places not accessible by train. This enables for in-depth study of the entire nation, from picturesque communities nestled in valleys to secret historical places.
- City buses: Major cities, such as Luxembourg City, have well-developed public bus networks that provide regular connections between important tourist locations and key areas of interest inside the city. Buses are an easy and economical method to move about.
- Regional buses provide a more exciting and picturesque approach to exploring. They link distant locations, allowing you to find hidden jewels and quaint communities off the usual road.
- Free Public Transport: All bus rides inside Luxembourg are free for passengers, same as railroads. This makes touring the country by bus an affordable way to explore its different offers.

International Flights and Major Airports

While Findel Airport is Luxembourg's principal international gateway, there are a few more airports in surrounding countries to consider based on your travel path and destination inside Luxembourg:
- Frankfurt Airport (FRA): Frankfurt Airport, located around 200 kilometers east of Luxembourg City in Germany, is a significant international hub. Connecting flights from Frankfurt to Luxembourg City are widely accessible, potentially providing a broader selection of flying options, particularly for long-distance travelers.
- Brussels Airport (BRU): Brussels Airport, located around 200 kilometers northwest of Luxembourg City in Belgium, is another alternative for connecting flights. Similar to Frankfurt, Brussels Airport has a broader number of foreign connections, perhaps giving you more options and flexibility when organizing your trip.
- Saarbrücken Airport (SCN) is a tiny regional airport located about 80 kilometers east of Luxembourg City, Germany. While just a few commercial flights depart from Saarbrücken, it might be a viable alternative for private aircraft or chartered flights.

Factors to consider while choosing flights:
- Consider your point of departure when booking flights. If you're traveling from a large European city, direct flights to Luxembourg Findel Airport may be accessible. For lengthier routes, connecting flights through Frankfurt, Paris, or Amsterdam may be required.
- Budget: Flight rates differ based on the airline, travel season, and booking period. Consider checking tickets from multiple airlines and booking your flights ahead of time to perhaps get better deals.
- Travel Time: Direct flights have the lowest travel time, however connecting flights might add hours to your journey. When making your selection, weigh the benefits of shorter travel times against the possibility of reduced rates.
- Airline Preferences: Some travelers may have preferences for certain airlines based on loyalty programs, onboard facilities, or previous experiences. Consider your airline preferences when considering flight alternatives.

PLANNING YOUR TRIP

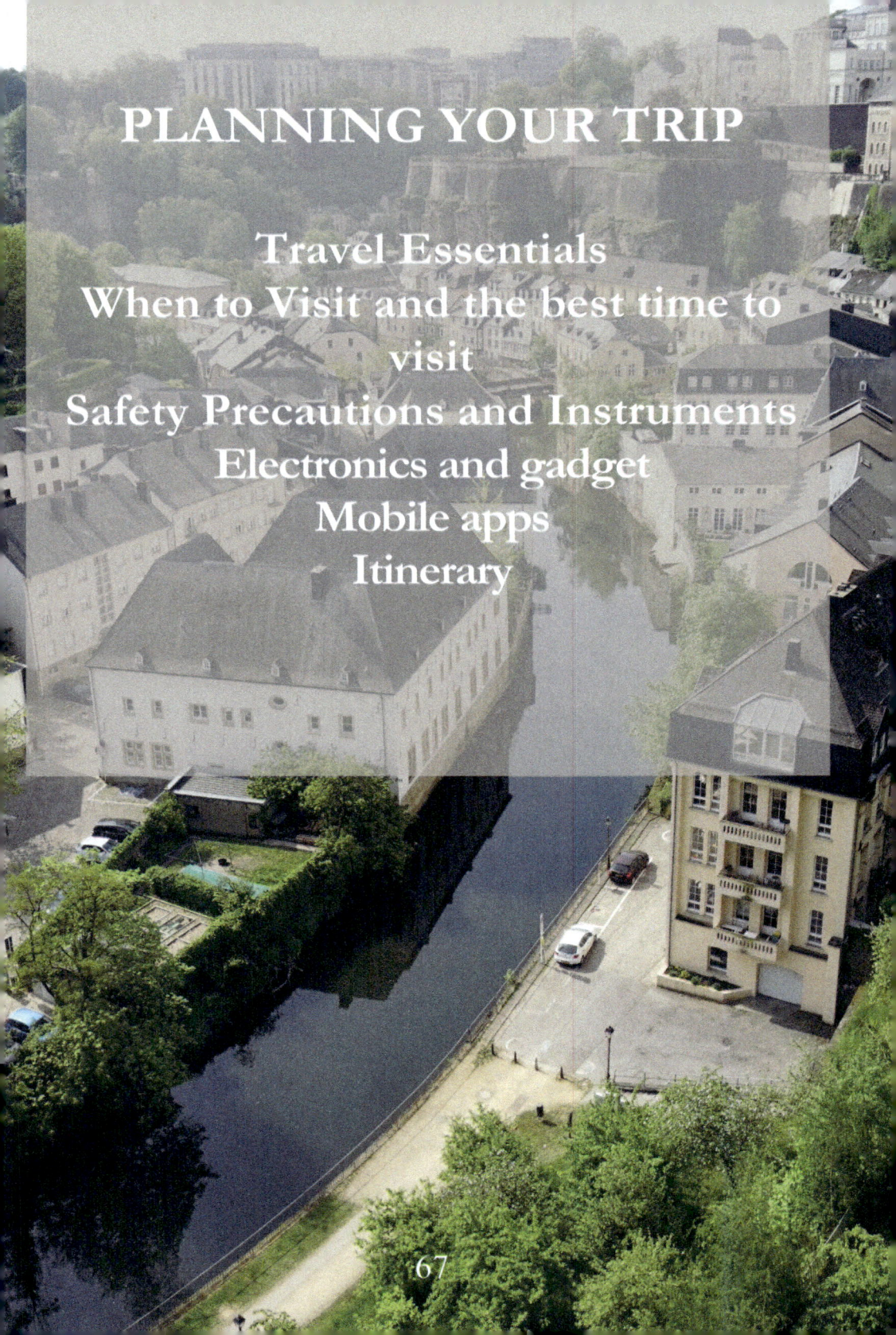

Travel Essentials
When to Visit and the best time to visit
Safety Precautions and Instruments
Electronics and gadget
Mobile apps
Itinerary

Travel Essentials

Luxembourg's weather may be unpredictable, with cold mornings and nights even during hot months. Layering helps you to respond to different emotions. For warmer days, use breathable materials such as cotton or linen, and for chilly evenings, add a light jacket or sweater.

Rainfall is a common occurrence in Luxembourg all year. A lightweight, packable raincoat or a foldable umbrella becomes an indispensable travel companion. On milder days, stylish raincoats may be worn as outerwear, allowing you to combine usefulness and design.

Comfortable walking shoes are essential for discovering scenic villages and traversing cobblestone streets. Consider wearing waterproof footwear on rainy days or while going off the usual route. An extra pair of comfy shoes is a useful companion for nights or museum visits.

Seasonal Nuances:

Spring (March-May): Pack layers to accommodate changing temperatures, remember your rain gear, and bring comfortable walking shoes.

Summer (June-August) is the season for light, airy apparel. Packing a swimsuit (for prospective water activities), sunglasses, a hat, and sunscreen is essential all year round, but especially during the summer months.

Autumn (September-November): As temperatures drop, layering becomes increasingly important. Bring a raincoat, scarf, and comfortable walking shoes for your adventures.

Winter (December-February): Dress warmly with a winter coat, gloves, a scarf, and sturdy shoes with adequate grip for snowy or ice weather. Thermal underwear may add a layer of warmth on very chilly days.

Important Documents and Electronics:
Ensure your passport is valid for your trip and at least six months after. If a visa is required, apply ahead of time. Keep digital or physical copies of your passport and travel insurance close by.

Bring your phone charger and a universal adapter to ensure compatibility with Luxembourg's electrical outlets (230V and plug types CEE 7/5 and CEE 7/7).

Consider carrying a camera to document your Luxembourgian experiences. If you're going to be touring for the day and need to keep your phone charged, a portable charger might come in handy.

Essentials
To reduce plastic waste, pack a reusable water bottle that you can refill during the day. Staying hydrated is critical, especially on expedition days.

Minor inconveniences should be treated with a simple first-aid pack containing important pharmaceuticals such as painkillers, allergy medication, and bandages.

Pack your normal toiletries, but keep in mind that baggage limitations apply while traveling. Consider travel-sized versions for further convenience and space savings.

While English is widely spoken in tourist regions, knowing a few simple words in Luxembourgish (Letzebuergesch) shows respect for the local culture. "Moien" (pronounced "moy-en") is a flexible greeting that may be used any time of the day. Many language learning applications make it easy to learn fundamental phrases while on the go. A comfy backpack is perfect for carrying necessities such as water, food, cameras, and guidebooks for day excursions or expeditions.

Religious locations need an appropriate dress. If you're unsure, cover your shoulders and knees.

While Luxembourg utilizes the Euro (EUR), consider converting some currency in advance for minor transactions or instances where card payments may not be accepted.

When to Visit and the best time to visit

Spring (March-May): Pros: Spring brings brilliant colors to Luxembourg, with blossoming wildflowers and a lush green landscape. There are fewer crowds than in the summer, providing a more relaxing experience. Hotel prices may be somewhat lower than in the high season.

Cons: The weather is variable, with periodic rain showers and cold mornings and nights. Some outdoor activities may be limited owing to the persistent winter chill.s.

Summer (June-August) has the most pleasant weather, with long sunny days and high temperatures perfect for outdoor activities. This is the main tourist season, with a vibrant atmosphere and several festivals and events.

Cons: Crowds can be large, particularly in famous tourist areas. Hotel prices are at their peak at this time.

Autumn (September-November): Pros: The season brings spectacular colors to Luxembourg, including flaming reds, golden yellows, and warm browns. The crowds begin to thin out, allowing for a more relaxing vacation experience, while hotel prices become more

cheaper than during the high season.
Cons: The weather may be unpredictable, with intermittent rain showers and cold temperatures. Some outdoor activities may be curtailed owing to the decreased daylight hours.

Winter (December to February):
Pros: Winter transforms Luxembourg into a paradise, with festive marketplaces adorned with lights and giving one-of-a-kind Christmas shopping options. Hotel prices are often at their lowest during this time.Cons: The weather may be very cold, with periodic snowfall and probable transport problems. The daylight hours are shorter, which limits outside exploring time.

The Best Time for You:
Outdoor adventurers: Spring, summer, and early fall provide wonderful weather for hiking, cycling, and enjoying the outdoors.
Festival Enthusiasts: Summer has the most vivid festivals and events, while winter brings the charm of Christmas markets.
Budget travelers: Spring and fall provide reduced hotel prices and a little less busy experience.
Tranquility Seekers: Consider traveling in early spring or late fall for a more relaxing and less crowded experience

The best time to visit Luxembourg is from spring to autumn, when the weather is mild and pleasant.

Safety Precautions and Instruments

General Safety:
Petty Theft Prevention: While petty theft is rare, vigilance is essential in congested locations such as public transit or tourist sites. Here are some preventive steps:
Use money belts or lockable crossbody purses for valuables.
Avoid overtly exhibiting costly jewelry or carrying large amounts of cash.
Keep a watch on your possessions, especially when sitting in cafés or restaurants.
Road Safety Awareness: Luxembourg's road network is well-maintained, however understanding the laws is essential:
Pedestrians: Always utilize the marked crossings and walkways. Follow traffic lights and remain alert to your surroundings.
Cyclists must wear helmets if they are under the age of 18, and they are highly advised for everyone. Use designated bike lanes wherever feasible. Respect traffic restrictions for your own and others' safety.
Nightlife Navigation:
Stick to Well-Lit Areas: While Luxembourg is typically safe at night, vigilance is advised. Choose well-lit roadways and avoid lonely or abandoned regions.
Plan and Inform: Before going out at night, notify your lodging or a trusted friend of your plans and approximate arrival time.

Emergency Preparedness:
Memorize the following emergency numbers: Police (112), Ambulance (112), and Fire Department (112). Keep these numbers in your phone for quick access.
Travel Insurance: Purchase travel insurance that includes medical crises, hospitalization, and trip cancellation/interruption. Ensure that the coverage is appropriate for your operations and potential hazards.
First-Aid Kit Essentials: Pack a simple first-aid kit containing pain pills, allergy medication, antiseptic wipes, and bandages to treat minor injuries while on the road.

Cybersecurity Measures:
Public Wi-Fi Caution: Public Wi-Fi networks are vulnerable to hacking. Avoid using public Wi-Fi to access sensitive information such as bank accounts or credit cards.
Consider utilizing a Virtual Private Network (VPN) to increase security while connecting to public Wi-Fi networks. A VPN encrypts your internet traffic, making it harder for criminals to steal your data.
Data backups: If your phone is lost or stolen, back up crucial travel papers such as images and passport scans to a second device. Cloud storage can also be a useful tool.

Essential Safety Instruments:
Travel paperwork: Keep your passport, travel insurance paperwork, and any relevant visas handy. Consider generating digital copies and keeping them separately incase the originals are lost.
Charged Mobile Phone: A properly charged mobile phone is essential for emergencies and navigation.

Luxembourg uses the Euro (EUR), with plug types CEE 7/5 and CEE 7/7. Include a universal adapter to ensure interoperability with your electrical gadgets.

A tiny flashlight or headlamp can be useful for navigating in low-light situations or during unexpected power outages.

Personal Alarm: Consider carrying a personal alarm as a deterrent in the event of a dangerous circumstance.

Additional tips for a safe journey:

Before traveling to Luxembourg, register with your home country's embassy or consulate. This permits them to reach you in the event of an emergency and give assistance as required.

Electronics and gadget

Smartphone: Your smartphone is a multi-purpose travel buddy. Use it for navigating using previously downloaded offline maps. Stay in touch with loved ones back home by phone, text, or video chat. Remember to verify your data roaming prices before leaving your local network.

Capture the splendor of Luxembourg with a high-quality camera. A tiny camera with a strong zoom is great for travel. If you plan to perform any outside activities, consider purchasing a waterproof camera. A portable charger will guarantee that you do not miss out on recording those memorable moments.

Luxembourg uses the Euro (EUR), with plug types CEE 7/5 and CEE 7/7. Pack a universal adapter to ensure compatibility with your electrical gadgets and prevent charging issues.

Power Bank: Bring a portable power bank to keep your smartphone and other critical gadgets charged while on the go, especially during long days of exploration.

Noise-Cancelling Headphones: Noise-cancelling headphones may be quite useful on public transit or while resting in cafés. They also allow you to focus just on music or podcasts.

E-reader: If you enjoy reading, an e-reader loaded with your favorite books might be a more space-efficient alternative to actual books. Consider downloading travel guides or e-books on Luxembourg to gain extra information during your stay.

A lightweight tripod may be a useful complement while photographing magnificent landscapes or at night.

It provides steadiness and enables you to take long-exposure shots without fuzzy results.

spare Camera Battery and Memory Cards: Carry a spare camera battery and memory cards to prevent missing out on important shots due to a dead battery or full memory.

Staying connected:

Mobile Hotspot: If you rely significantly on internet access and your phone plan does not provide reasonable data roaming, try renting a mobile hotspot in Luxembourg. This lets you connect several devices to the internet for a set charge.

Portable Wi-Fi Router: If you're traveling with a group, a portable Wi-Fi router might be an inexpensive way to share an internet connection among your companions.

While a universal adapter provides compatibility with Luxembourg's plugs, a travel converter might also be useful if you want to visit other countries during your vacation with differing voltage requirements.

Luggage Scale: To avoid extra baggage penalties at the airport, use a luggage scale ahead of time to verify your suitcase does not exceed the weight limit.

📱 Mobile apps

Mobilitéit.lu: The official app from Luxembourg's public transport agency is a need. It gives real-time information on buses, trains, and trams, such as route planning, travel schedules, and anticipated delays.

The CFL smartphone app, provided by Luxembourg's national railway corporation, includes full train timetables, ticket transactions, and live train tracking functionality.

CityApp - Your Guide to VDL: This complete software allows you to explore Luxembourg City, a dynamic city. It provides interactive maps, point-of-interest information, and even self-guided walking tours to help you discover hidden gems.

LuxTrust Mobile: This app is required for residents and may be useful for regular visits. It enables users to access secure online services and capabilities offered by the Luxembourg government and other entities.

S-Net Mobile: This app is provided by the national power supplier, Société Luxembourgeoise de Navigation Aérienne (SNT). While not required for most guests, it might be useful for individuals staying in self-catering lodgings to monitor power use and report problems.

LALUX easyAPP: If you have insurance or other financial products with LALUX, their mobile app allows you to manage your policies, monitor claims, and access critical information while on the move.

MyGuichet.lu: The Luxembourg government's official app provides information on administrative procedures and public services, as well as the ability to arrange appointments for specific services.

WEBTAXI: This app allows for easy cab booking throughout Luxembourg. It lets you hail a cab, follow its arrival in real-time, and even pay for your journey cashlessly through the app.

Tandem: This language exchange software allows you to connect with native Luxembourgish speakers. Improve your conversational abilities, learn about local culture, and perhaps meet language partners to make your vacation more enjoyable.

Aurelux: This software provides an interactive approach to learning Luxembourgish. It mixes audio lectures, flashcards, and gamified components to make language learning more enjoyable and successful.

Babbel/Duolingo: While not Luxembourg-specific, these popular language learning apps include courses in French and German, Luxembourg's two official languages. Learning basic words in these languages can improve your communication skills and overall experience.

HelloFresh: If you're staying in self-catering accommodation and enjoy cooking on occasion, HelloFresh delivers pre-portioned meal kits with fresh ingredients and simple recipes directly to your door.

The Schueberfouer App allows you to immerse yourself in the colorful Schueberfouer fair during the summer months. It includes a schedule of activities, information about rides and attractions, and the ability to purchase ride tickets in advance.

Selecting the Right Apps:
Identify your needs. Consider your travel style, hobbies, and planned activities while selecting the applications that will best meet your needs.

Offline Functionality: For circumstances when internet connectivity is limited, choose applications that include offline functionality such as downloading maps or storing itineraries.

Data Usage: If you often use apps outside of your home network, keep in mind that data roaming costs may apply. Consider using public Wi-Fi or getting a local SIM card with a data package.

📋 Itinerary

On Day 1, explore the Bock Casemates and learn about their historical significance.
Explore the picturesque Grund district and enjoy local dishes at a historic eatery.
Day 2: Tour the National Museum of History and Art.
Explore the Luxembourg City History Museum to learn more about the city's past.
Visit the MUDAM (Museum of Modern Art) to view modern art from Luxembourg and throughout the world.
Experience the Clausen district's active nightlife, which includes fashionable pubs and restaurants.
Day 3: Take a day excursion to the Moselle Valley, known for its wineries and picturesque towns.
Explore Grevenmacher, a lovely village with a rich winemaking culture.
Indulge in a wine-tasting session at a local winery, where you may savor the region's outstanding wines.
Enjoy a picturesque boat tour down the Moselle River, taking in the valley's stunning views.
Day 4: Visit Vianden, a lovely village in the Ardennes region.
Explore the magnificent Vianden Castle, a stunning 11th-century building. Explore the great halls and delve.into its history.
Exit the castle and explore the picturesque village of Vianden.
Stroll through the tiny alleys, dotted with charming shops and cafés, taking in the town's medieval atmosphere.

Consider visiting the Victor Hugo House, a museum devoted to the renowned French writer who sought asylum in Vianden.

Day 5: Spend the day touring the Mullerthal area, widely known as Luxembourg's Little Switzerland. This place is ideal for wildlife lovers.

Hike the Schwanzfels Trail, one of the region's most popular paths, which offers breathtaking views and natural treasures. Explore the several smaller paths for a more private experience.

Consider visiting the Schulenburg, which is a natural amphitheater built from the rock wall.

Day 6: Have a leisurely breakfast at a local cafe and explore the city center at your speed.

The Jardins de la Pétrusse, the city's oldest park, offers a calm escape.

Day 7: Depending on your departure schedule, have a farewell breakfast at a nearby cafe. Do some last-minute souvenir buying or return to a favorite site from your trip. Bid farewell to Luxembourg, taking with you fond memories of your fantastic experience.

ACOMMODATION

Hostels
Campgrounds
Affordable and Budget-Friendly hotels
Luxury Hotels
Family Hotels
Romatic Hotels

Hostels

Youth Hostel Luxembourg City

Location: 2 Rue du Fort Olisy, Luxembourg City 2261 Luxembourg
Contact: (+352) 26 27 66 200
Email address: info@youthhostels.lu
Price range: £38-$39

Youth Hostel Vianden

Location: 3 Montee du Chateau, Vianden 9408 Luxembourg
Contact: (+352) 26 27 66 800
Email address: vianden@youthhostels.lu
Price range: £36

Youth Hostel Larochette

Location: 45 Rue Osterbour, Larochette 7622 Luxembourg
Contact: (+352) 26 27 66 550
Email address: larochette@youthhostels.lu
Price range: £36

Youth Hostel Beaufort

Location: 55 Route de Dillingen, Beaufort 6315 Luxembourg
Contact: (+352) 26 27 66 300
Email address: beaufort@youthhostels.lu
Price range: £36

Youth Hostel Lultzhausen

Location: 20 An Der Driicht, Lultzhausen 9666 Luxembourg
Contact: (+352) 26 27 66 600
Email address: lultzhausen@youthhostels.lu
Price range: £33 - £34

Camp grounds

Camping KAUL

Location: 46b Rue Joseph Simon, Wiltz 9550 Luxembourg
Contact: (+352) 950 3591
Email address: info@kaul.lu
Price range: £106 - £129

Camping Berkel

Location: 5 Op Der Millen, Bockholtzermillen 9637 Luxembourg
Contact: (+352) 83 90 54
Email address: info@campingberkel.com
Price range: £54 - £66

Camping Officiel Echternach

Location: 17 Route de Diekirch, Echternach 6430 Luxembourg
Contact: (+352) 72 02 72
Email address: camping@visitechternach.lu
Price range: £45 - £82

Camping Um Bierg

Location: 32 Um Bierg Tarchamps, 9689 Luxembourg
Contact: (+352) 621 397 620
Email address: info@umbierg.lu
Price range: £69 - £117

Camping Belle-Vue 2000

Location: 29 Rue de Consdorf, Berdorf 6551 Luxembourg
Contact: (+352) 621 397 620
Email address: info@umbierg.lu.
Price range: £88 - £164

Affordable and Budget friendly hotels

Hotel Bristol

Location: 11 Rue de Strasbourg, Luxembourg City 2561 Luxembourg
Contact: (+352) 48 58 30
Email address: contact@hotel-bristol.lu
Price range: £124 - £163

The hotel is in the center of the city, rooms are nice and clean. The location of the hotel is perfect in walking distance from the historical part of the city.

Ibis Budget Luxembourg Sud

Location: Rue De Turi, Livange, Livange, Luxembourg, L-3378
Contact: (+352) 26 51 86
Email address: H6768@accor.com
Price range: £68 - £90

The ibis budget Luxembourg Sud is within 15 minutes from the Findel airport (E44, luxair). Ibis Budget Luxembourg Sud is an excellent choice for travelers, offering a family-friendly environment alongside many helpful amenities designed to enhance your stay.

Le Petit Poete

Location: 13 Place du Marche, Echternach 6460 Luxembourg
Contact: (+352) 72 00 72 1
Email address: contact@lepetitpoete.lu.
Price range: £124 - £146

Excellent location, impeccable cleanliness, and really pleasant owners and staff!

Ibis Luxembourg Sud

Location: Rue de Turi, Roeser 3378 Luxembourg
Contact: (+352) 26 52 01.
Email address: H5587@accor.com. C
Price range: £89 - £113

Cafe Hotel de Ville de Bruxelles

Location: 15 Grand-Rue, Vianden 9410 Luxembourg
Contact: (+352) 26 87 47 50
Email address: hotel-cafevilledebruxelles@hotmail.com
Price range: £54- £60

Hotel Brasserie Nagel

Location: 2 Route de Bettel, Vianden 9415 Luxembourg
Contact: (+352) 83 45 05
Email address: info@camping-vianden.lu
Price range: £92- £93

LUXURY HOTELS

Sofitel Luxembourg Europe

Location: 4 Rue du Fort Niedergruenewald Quartier européen Nord, Plateau de Kirchberg, Luxembourg City 2226 Luxembourg
Contact: (+352) 43 77 61
Email address: H1314@sofitel.com
Price range: £177 - £262

Le Royal Hotels & Resorts

Location: 12 Boulevard Royal, Luxembourg City 2449 Luxembourg
Contact: (+352) 2-416161
Email address: reservation-lux@leroyal.com
Price range: £211 - £261

Le Place d'Armes Hotel

Location: 18 Place d'Armes Grand Duché de Luxembourg, Luxembourg City 1136 Luxembourg
Contact: (+352) 27 47 37
Email address: info@hotel-leplacedarmes.com
Price range: £268 - £409

Meliá Luxembourg

Location: 1 Park Drai Eechelen 10 Rue Fort Thuengen, Luxembourg City 1499 Luxembourg
Contact: (+352) 27333 1
Email address: melia.luxembourg@melia.
Price range: £143 - £202

Park Inn Hotel

Location: Avenue De La Gare 45-47, Luxembourg City 1611 Luxembourg
Contact: (+352) 26 89 18 1
Email address: info.luxembourg@parkinn.com
Price range: £127 - £193

Novotel Luxembourg Centre

Location: 35 Rue du Laboratoire, Luxembourg City 1911 Luxembourg
Contact: (+352) 24 87 81
Email address: H5556@accor.com
Price range: £128 - £206

Grand Hotel Cravat

Location: 29 Boulevard F-D Roosevelt, Luxembourg City 2450 Luxembourg
Contact: (+352) 22 19 75 1
Email address: contact@hotelcravat.lu
Price range: £137 - £197

FAMILY HOTELS

Hostellerie du Grunewald

Location: 10-14 Route d'Echternach, Luxembourg City 1453 Luxembourg
Contact: (+352) 24 51 49 20
Email address: info@hdg.lu
Price range: £90 - £156

Hotel NH Luxembourg

Location: 1 Route de Treves, Luxembourg City 2633 Luxembourg
Contact: (+352) 34 0571
Email address: nhluxembourg@nh-hotels.com
Price range: £90 - £154

Sieweburen

Location: 36 Rue des Sept-Fontaines, Luxembourg City 2534 Luxembourg
Contact: (+352) 44 23 56
Email address: info@sieweburen.lu
Price range: £113 - £155

City Hotel

Location: 1 Rue de Strasbourg / Coin Avenue de la Liberte 1 rue de Strasbourg, Luxembourg City 2561 Luxembourg
Contact: (+352) 29 11 22
Email address: mail@cityhotel.lu
Price range: £127 - £186

Hotel Simoncini

Location: 6 Rue Notre-Dame, Luxembourg City 2240 Luxembourg
Contact: (+352) 22 28 44
Email address: simoncinihotel@pt.lu
Price range: £127 - £186

Les Jardins d'Anaïs Hôtel

Location: 2 Place Sainte Cunegonde, Luxembourg City 1367 Luxembourg
Contact: (+352) 28 99 80 00
Email address: reservation@jardinsdanais.lu
Price range: £174 - £248

Hotel Pax Luxembourg

Location: 121 Route de Thionville, Luxembourg City 2611 Luxembourg
Contact: (+352) 48 25 63
Email address: info@hotelpax.lu
Price range: £94 - £137

ROMATIC HOTELS

Hotel Parc Beaux-Arts

Location: 1 Rue Sigefroi, Luxembourg City 2536 Luxembourg
Contact: (+352) 26 86 76 1
Email address: reception.beauxarts@goereshotels.com
Price range: £194 - £254

DoubleTree by Hilton

Location: 12 Rue Jean Engling, Luxembourg City 1466 Luxembourg
Contact: (+352) 43 78 05 8
Email address: reservation@doubletree-luxembourg.com
Price range: £82 - £135

Hôtel Perrin

Location: 9 Rue de Strasbourg, Luxembourg City 2561 Luxembourg
Contact: (+352) 29 96 60
Email address: hello@perrin.lu
Price range: £100 - £163

INNSiDE by Meliá

Location: 12 Rue Henri M. Schnadt, Luxembourg City 2530 Luxembourg
Contact: (+352) 28 84 53 1
Email address: innside.luxembourg@melia.com
Price range: £106 - £172

Parc Hotel Alvisse

Location: 120 Route d'Echternach, Luxembourg City 1453 Luxembourg
Contact: (+352) 43 56 43
Email address: info@parc-hotel.lu
Price range: £90 - £137

Hotel Vauban

Location: 10 Place Guillaume II, Luxembourg City 1648 Luxembourg
Contact: (+352) 22 04 93
Email address: info@hotelvauban.lu
Price range: £129 - £173

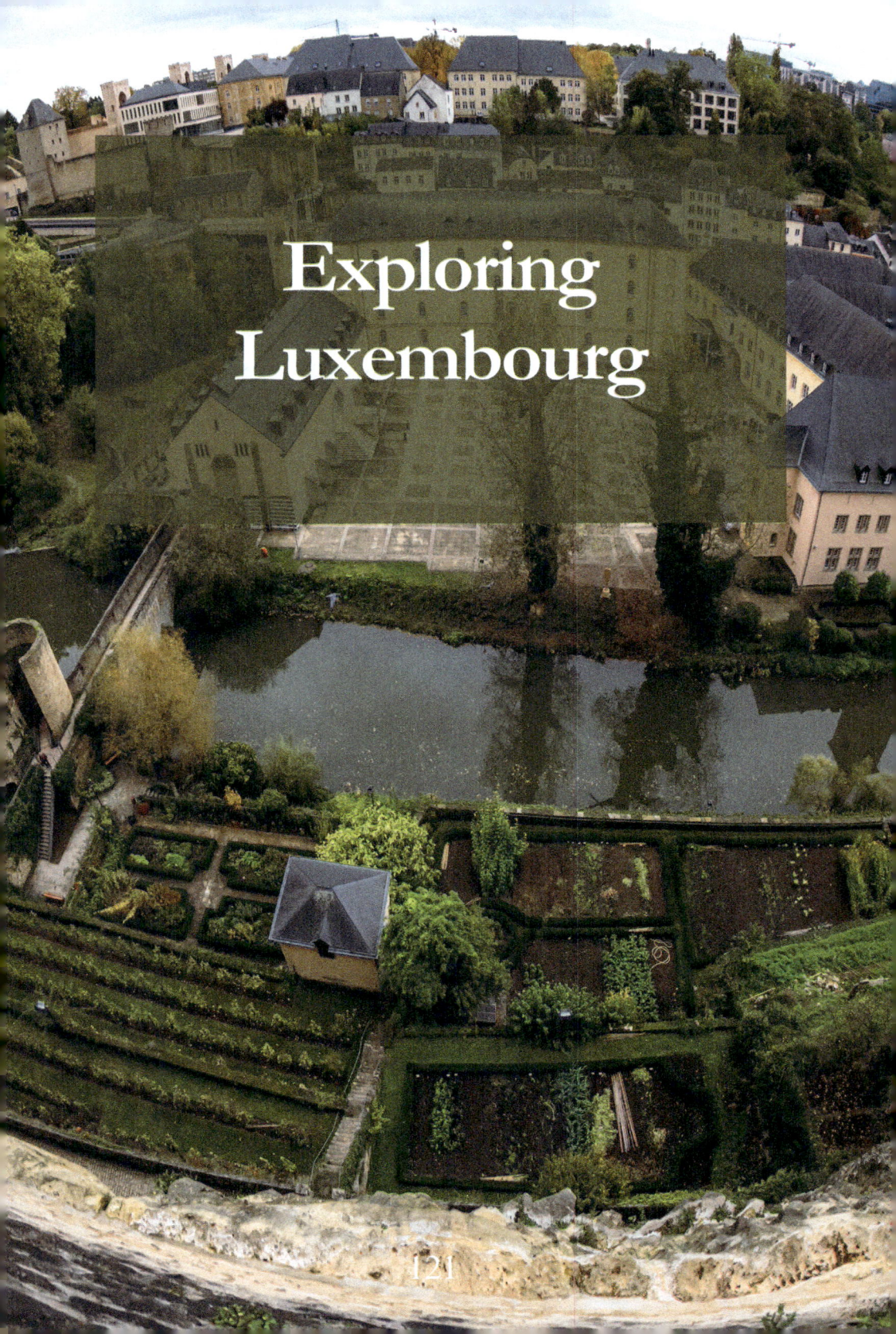

Exploring Luxembourg

Tours and activities

Luxembourg city walking tour

Price range: From £27.55 per adult
Ages 4-75, max of 13 per group
Duration: 2hours
Contact number: +1 855 275 5071

Luxembourg city walking and wine tasting tour

Price range: From £38.57 per adult
Ages 4-90, max of 12 per group
Duration: 2hours
Contact number: +1 855 275 5071

e-Scavenger hunt Luxembourg

Price range: From £34.16 per adult
Ages 0-120, max of 6 per group
Duration: 2hours
Contact number: +1 855 275 5071

Luxembourg Guided Walking Tour in the city

Price range: From £38.57 per adult
Ages 0-99, max of 15 per group
Duration: 2hours 30 minutes
Contact number: +1 855 275 5071

Luxembourg City Guided E-bike Tour

Price range: From £67.23 per adult
Ages 4-99, max of 15 per group
Duration: 3hours
Contact number: +1 855 275 5071

Private Historic Battle of the Bulge Sites Full-Day Tour

Price range: From £593.85 per adult
Ages 16-75
Duration: 8–10 hours
Contact number: +1 855 275 5071

City Train Tour in the old town of Luxembourg

Price range: From £15.98 per adult
Ages 0-90, max of 45 per group
Duration: 45 minutes
Contact number: +1 855 275 5071

Luxembourg Moselle Day Tour with wine tasting

Price range: From £109.11 per adult
Ages 0-99, max of 19 per group
Duration: 8 hours
Contact number: +1 855 275 5071

Luxembourg private 1-day tour

Price range: From £578.59 per adult
Ages 12-75
Duration: 8 hours
Contact number: +1 855 275 5071

Top attractions

Vianden Castle
Location: Montee du Chateau, Vianden 9401 Luxembourg
Contact number: +352 83 41 08 1
Email: info@castle-vianden.lu

Luxembourg American Cemetery Memorial
Location: 50 Val du Scheid, Luxembourg City 2517 Luxembourg
Contact number: +352 43 17 27
Email: luxembourg@abmc.gov

Le Chemin de la Corniche

Location: Chemin de la Corniche, Luxembourg City 1339 Luxembourg

The Cornich is one spot in Luxembourg that everyone should see. The stroll along this bridge is really breathtaking, especially at night. It provides a magnificent perspective of the ancient city and surrounds.

Mullerthal Trail
Location: Luxembourg's B.P. 152 L-6402 Echternach Grand-Duché de Luxembourg
Contact number: +352 72 04 57-1, +352 72 75 24
Email: info@mullerthal.lu.

Cathédrale Notre-Dame
Location: Rue Notre-Dame, Luxembourg City 2240 Luxembourg
Contact number: +352 44 74 34 01
Email: notre-dame@cathol.lu

Grund

Location: Grund, Luxembourg City 1238 Luxembourg
Contact number: +352 22 28 09
Email: touristinfo@lcto.lu

MNHM National Museum of Military History
Location: National Museum of Military History Diekirch 10, Rue Bamertal L-9209 Diekirch
Contact number: +352 80 89 08
Email: reception@mnhm.lu

Bofferding

Location: 2 Boulevard JF Kennedy, Bascharage 4930 Luxembourg
Contact number: +352 23 63 64 217
Email: visite@bofferding.lu

Grand Ducal Palace
Location: Grand Ducal Palace 17, rue du Marché-aux-Herbes L-1728 Luxembourg City
Contact number: +352 22 28 09
Email: touristinfo@lcto.lu

Iconic sites and land marks

Casemates du Bock

Location: Montée de Clausen, Luxembourg City 1343 Luxembourg

Contact number: +352 22 28 09

Email: touristinfo@lcto.lu

Pfaffenthal Lift

Location: 2 Rue du Pont, Luxembourg City 2344 Luxembourg
Contact number: +35247962310

The elevator runs every day from 5.45 in the morning until 1 o' clock at night.
Every first monday of the month, the elevator is out of order due to maintenance (from 9.00 am till 5.45 am the following day).

Place d'Armes
Location: Place d'Armes, Luxembourg City 1136 Luxembourg

If you want somewhere to chill out and watch the passing scenery this is the place to go.

Place de la Constitution
Location: 2 Bd. Franklin Delano Roosevelt, Luxembourg City 1116 Luxembourg
Contact number: +352 22 28 09
A location that gives amazing views of the city. definitely a place to view - there you can meet tourists and locals alike, while they walk around the area

Statue de la Grande Duchesse Charlotte
Location: Place de Clairefontaine, Luxembourg City
1341 Luxembourg

A fine square to visit and see the statue of the Grand Duchess. The building around the square are remarkable to see and know some of the history.

Town Hall
Location: Place Guillaume II, Luxembourg City 2090 Luxembourg
Contact number: +352 47 961

This is a beautiful French style building. There are cafes and bars around. You should not miss it on your vacation!

Stierchen Bridge

Location: Rue Sosthene Weis, Luxembourg City 1343 Luxembourg

It's a nice little bridge. There is an amazing view when crossing this bridge. It is a must seen place in Luxembourg.

Museums / Hidden gems

Nationalmusée um Fëschmaart

Location: Marché-aux-Poissons, Luxembourg City 2345 Luxembourg

Contact number: +352 47 93 30 1

This is Luxembourg's main art and history museum. Right at the capital's historic downtown, it is a large place to understand the country from prehistory to contemporary development.

Lëtzebuerg City Museum

Location: 14, rue du Saint-Esprit, Luxembourg City 1475 Luxembourg
Contact number: +352 47 96 45 00

The building is beautifully designed, making full use of the natural features. Very informative using a range of exhibits to demonstrate the full history of the city from earliest times to the present day in a fair and balanced way.

National Museum of Natural History

Location: 25 Rue Munster, Luxembourg City 2160 Luxembourg
Contact number: +352 46 22 33 1

There are lots of great exhibits and a very calm environment and very creatively design. A lot to see even for little kids.

Fort Thungen

Location: 3 Park Drai Eechelen, Luxembourg City 1499 Luxembourg
Contact number: +352 26 43 35

It is a nice historic site and one of the many fortifications in and around Luxemburg

Tramway and Bus Museum

Location: 63 Rue de Bouillon, Luxembourg City 1248 Luxembourg
Contact number: +352 47 96 23 85

It is a Nice museum which demonstrates the history of Tramway and busses. They also have good collections which kids would enjoy a lot.

Am Tunnel (BCEE Bâtiment Rousegaertchen)

Location: 16, rue Zithe, Luxembourg City 2954 Luxembourg
Contact number: +352 40 15 24 50

Mudam Luxembourg Modern Art Museum

Location: 3 Park Drai Eechelen, Luxembourg City 1499 Luxembourg
Contact number: +352 45 37 85 1

A fantastic building with great exhibits. Nice spaces to facilitate the appreciation of the artworks on display.

The Bank Museum

Location: 1 Place de Metz, Luxembourg City 1930 Luxembourg

This museum gives a good overview of the banking system and how things have changed over the years in terms of technology

Nature and parks

Parc Merveilleux

Location: route de Mondorf, Bettembourg 3260 Luxembourg

Contact number: +352 51 10 48 1

Very nice park with interesting animals. There are lot of options to play for kids

Playground Avenue Monterey

Location: 45 Avenue Monterey, Luxembourg City 2163 Luxembourg
Contact number: +352 47 96 34 23

It is a great family playround to relax on a bench or take a stroll among the trees, and a place where children can have a great time on the swings.

Gaalgebierg, Le Parc Municipal Escher Déierepark Escher Bamhaiser

Location: 64 Gaalgebierg, Esch-sur-Alzette 4142 Luxembourg
Contact number: +352 27 54 37 50

It is a nice animal park with beautiful creaturesThe playground is clean and provides lots of space for kids.

Echternach Lake

Location: Rue des Romains, Echternach 6578 Luxembourg

Contact number: +352 72 02 88

This is a great location for a walk, the lake is very beautiful and also the countryside and surrounding areas are all lovely.

Pétrusse Parks

Location: Vallée de la Pétrusse, Luxembourg City 1930 Luxembourg

It is a beautiful park in the city, a very good place to spend time with your family and friends or go for a walk to enjoy the nature

Schiessentumpel Waterfall
Location: CR121, Mullerthal 6245 Luxembourg
Contact number: +352 87 89 88

Nice waterfall and very scenic. Worth a visit

Edmund Klein Park

Location: 1 Rue Pierre d'Aspelt, 1142 Ville-Haute Luxembourg

Beautiful park for relaxation and nice walk. Fresh air, smell of the trees and grass.

Moselle Valley

Location: 52 Route du Vin, 5405 Bech-Kleinmacher Schengen, Luxembourg
Contact number: +352 26 74 78 74
The Moselle valley is very beautifull, Serene , picturesque and colourful. Worth a visit

Fun and games

Crocus Quest Games

Location: 14 Rue Robert Stumper, Luxembourg City 2557 Luxembourg
Contact number: +352 621 689 882

A great fun escape room with different and unique challenges, Good puzzles and so much more! worth a visit

den Nordpool

Location: Rue de l'Ecole, Colmar-Berg 7730 Luxembourg
Contact number: +352 83 55 43 342

Enigmo Rooms

Location: 203 Rue du Parc Rez-de-chaussée, Dudelange 3542 Luxembourg
Contact number: +352 621 496 639

It is an absolutely unique outdoor escape experience. Worth a visit!

216k Escape Room

Location: 59 Rue de Cessange, Luxembourg City 1320 Luxembourg
Contact number: +352 621 142 020

It is a great escape room with an eye for detail and great story telling.

Nightlife Activities

Ratelach

Location: 116 Rue de Luxembourg Au fond de la cour, à gauche, Esch-sur-Alzette 4221 Luxembourg
Contact number: +352 661 554 477

Great place to go and have a quiet glass of wine or listen to some live music

den Atelier

Location: 54 Rue de Hollerich, Luxembourg City 1740 Luxembourg
Contact number: +352 49 54 85 1

A very nice club with near stage, cool and average sound quality

De Gudde Wëllen

Location: 17, Rue Du Saint Esprit, Luxembourg City 1475 Luxembourg
Contact number: +35226202886

Perfectly located for a last drink before taking the late night train.

Bar:Bar

Location: 14 Rue de la Boucherie, Luxembourg City 1247 Luxembourg
Contact number: +352 661 909 185

Awesome cocktail bar in Luxembourg

The White Rose Pub

Location: 7 Rue Dicks Tramstop Place de Paris, Luxembourg City 1417 Luxembourg
Contact number: +352 661 379 458

Friendly, cosy and affordable pub

Spas and wellness

Cabinet Jason Edwards

Location: 54 Rue de la Forêt, Luxembourg City 1534 Luxembourg
Contact number: +352 691 412 266

Very good massage service. The massages significantly reduce muscle tensions.

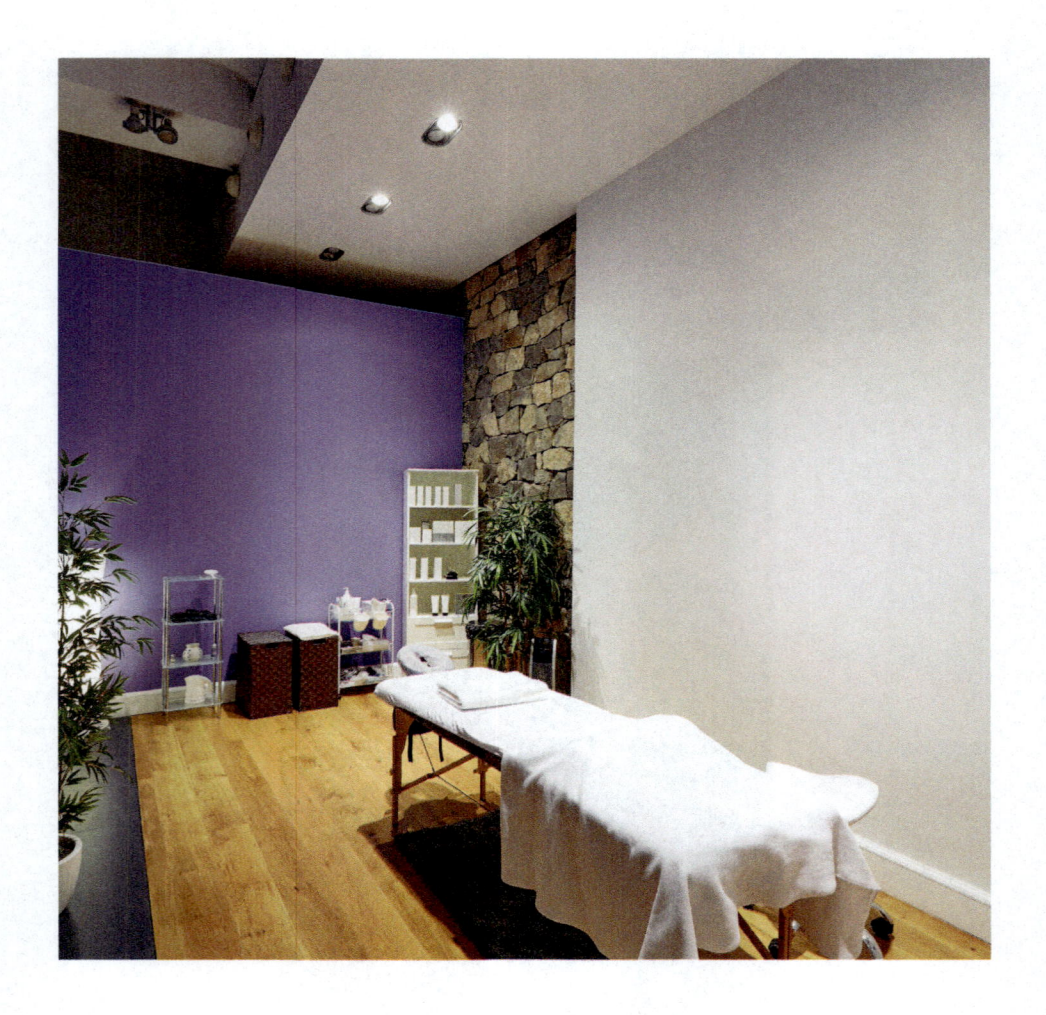

De Masseur

Location: 20 Avenue de la Faiencerie, Luxembourg City 1510 Luxembourg
Contact number: +352 26 10 34 34

It is one of the best place for a massage in luxembourg!

Siam Thai Massage

Location: 72 Grand-Rue, Luxembourg City 1660 Luxembourg
Contact number:+352 26 47 89 47

Excellent place for a thai traditional massage

Saint-Nicolas Spa

Location: 31 Esplanade, Remich 5533 Luxembourg
Contact number: +352 26 663

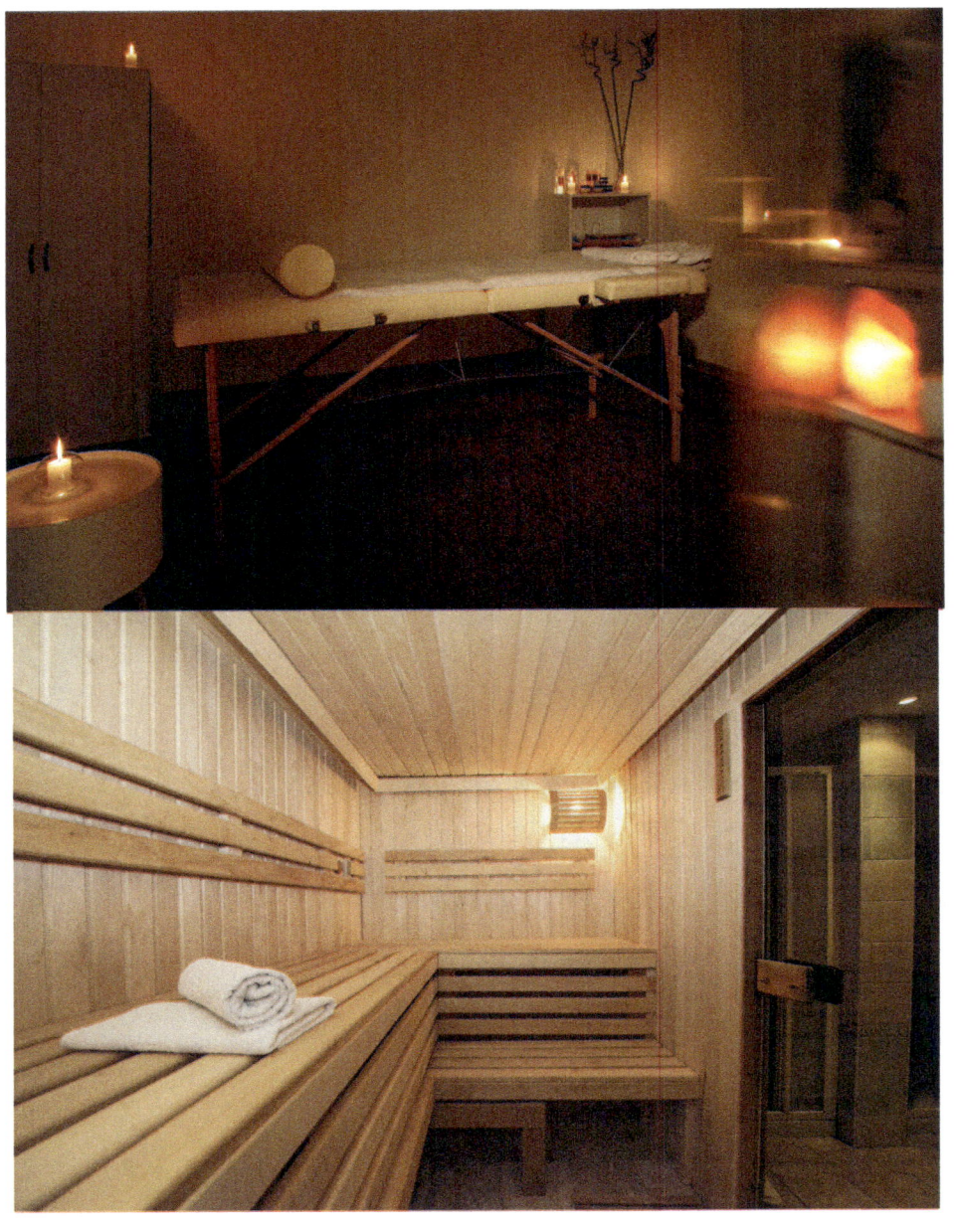

Sun Massages Luxembourg

Location: 1 Place Francois-Joseph Dargent, Luxembourg City 1413 Luxembourg
Contact number: +352 691 860 267

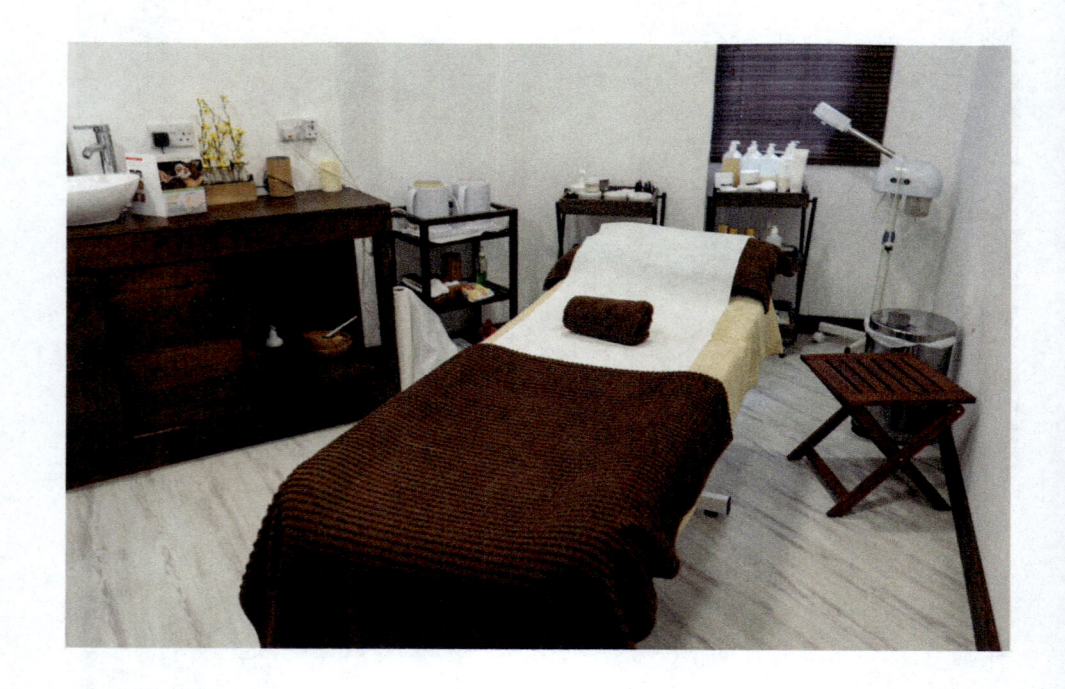

Shows and concerts activities

Philharmonie Luxembourg
Location: 1 Place de l'Europe, Luxembourg City 1499 Luxembourg
Contact number: : +352 26 32 26 32

Casino Luxembourg

Location: 41 Rue Notre-Dame, Luxembourg City 2240 Luxembourg

Contact number: : +352 22 50 45

They have a really good show and also it is very enjoyable. Casino is really good and worth a visit.

Grand Théâtre de la Ville de Luxembourg

Location: 1 Rond-Point Robert Schuman, Luxembourg City 2525 Luxembourg
Contact number: : +352 47 96 39 00

This is a great place for culture and entertainment

Théâtre des Capucins

Location: 9 Place du Theatre, Luxembourg City 2613 Luxembourg

Contact number: : +352 47 96 39 00

Théâtre Municipal
Location: 122 Rue de l'Alzette, Esch-sur-Alzette 4010 Luxembourg
Contact number: : +352 47 96 39 00

Carlitos Comedy Club

Location: 65 Rue du Fort Neipperg, Luxembourg City L-2230 Luxembourg
Contact number: : +352 621 322 882

RESTAURANT
Local cuisine
Fine dining/Romantic
Budget friendly
Coffe and tea
Bars and Pubs

Local cuisine

Restaurant Um Dierfgen

Location: 6 Cote d'Eich 40 métres du parking du Théâtre, Luxembourg City 1450 Luxembourg

Contact number: : +352 22 61 41

Special diets: Vegetarian Friendly

Meals: Lunch and dinner

This resturant is known for their best Luxembourgish cuisine and hospitality

Bick Stuff

Location: 95 Rue de Clausen, Luxembourg City 1342 Luxembourg
Contact number: : +352 26 09 47 31
Meals: Lunch and dinner

Clairefontaine

Location: 9 Place de Clairefontaine, Luxembourg City 1341 Luxembourg
Contact number: : +352 46 22 11
Meals: Lunch and dinner
Special diets: Vegetarian Friendly, Vegan Options, Gluten Free Options

This restuarant have great food, excellent wine and brilliant service. It is a must visit

Cyrano
Location: 22 Rue du Laboratoire, Luxembourg City 1911 Luxembourg
Contact number: : +352 27 48 90 87
Meals: Lunch, Dinner, Drinks
Special diets: Vegetarian Friendly, Vegan Options, Gluten Free Options

Rotisserie Ardennaise
Location: 1 Avenue du DIX Septembre, Luxembourg City 2551 Luxembourg
Contact number: : +352 45 09 74
Meals:Dinner, Drinks, Lunch

Bosso

Location: 18 Rue Munster, Luxembourg City 2160 Luxembourg
Contact number: : +352 26 20 04 49
Meals:Lunch, Dinner, Late Night, Drinks
Special diets: Vegetarian Friendly, Vegan Options, Gluten Free Options

Fine dining/Romantic

Le Sud

Location: 8 Rives de Clausen, Luxembourg City 2165 Luxembourg
Contact number: : +352 26 47 87 50
Meals: Lunch, Dinner, Late Night
Special diets: Vegetarian Friendly, Vegan Options, Gluten Free Options

Le Laboratoire

Location: 1 Rue des Trevires parking Rocade en dessous, Luxembourg City 2628 Luxembourg
Contact number: : +352 27 48 97 07
Meals: Lunch, Dinner, Drinks

Radici

Location: 6 Rue du Fort Niedergruenewald Sofitel Luxembourg Europe, Luxembourg City 2226 Luxembourg
Contact number: : +352 43 77 68 70
Meals: Dinner, Late Night, Drinks
Special diets: Vegetarian Friendly, Vegan Options

Terra Steakhouse

Location: 15 Rue Edward Steichen, Luxembourg City 2540 Luxembourg
Contact number: : +352 28 80 23 63
Meals: Lunch, Dinner, Drinks

Mosconi

Location: 13 Rue Munster, Luxembourg City 2160 Luxembourg
Contact number: : +352 54 69 94
Meals: Lunch, Dinner, Late Night
Special diets: Vegetarian Friendly, Gluten Free Options

Le Bouquet Garni

Location: 32 Rue de l'Eau, Luxembourg City 1449 Luxembourg
Contact number: : +352 26 20 06 20
Meals:Lunch, Dinner, Late Night
Special diets: Vegetarian Friendly

Budget Friendly Restaurant

Aka Cite

Location: 3 Rue Genistre, Luxembourg City 1623 Luxembourg
Contact number: : +352 20 33 22 45
Meals: Lunch, Dinner, Late Night, Drinks
Special diets: Vegetarian Friendly, Vegan Options, Gluten Free Options

Lux'Burgers

Location: 17 Rue de Bonnevoie, Luxembourg City 1260 Luxembourg
Contact number: : +352 26 19 00 70
Meals: Lunch, Dinner
Special diets: Vegetarian Friendly

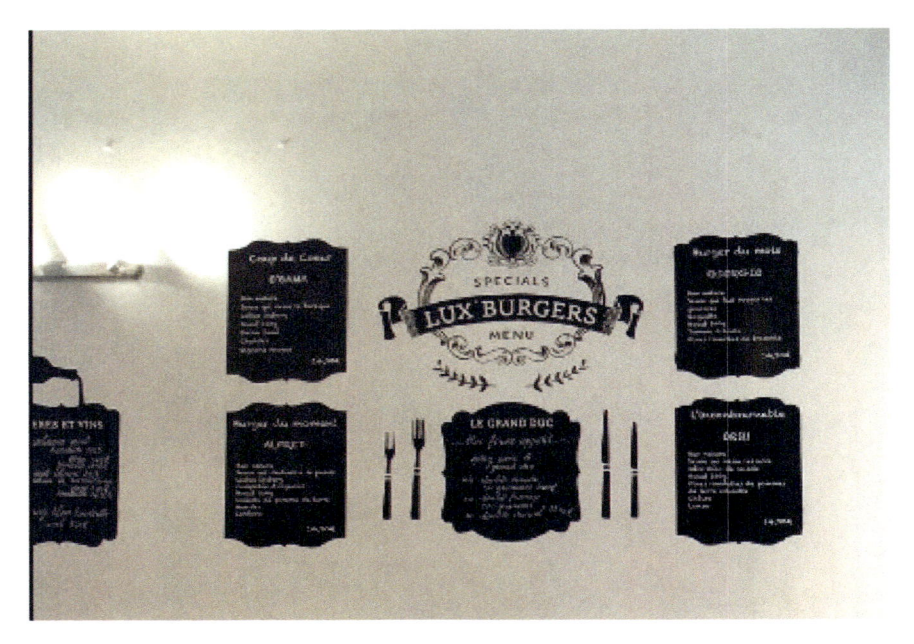

Dans le Noir ? Luxembourg
Location: 6 Rue du Fort Niedergruenewald Au sein du Novotel Luxembourg Kirchberg, Luxembourg City 2226 Luxembourg
Contact number: : +352 42 98 48 1
Meals: Dinner

Restaurant New Delhi
Location: 165 Muehlenweg, Luxembourg City 2155 Luxembourg
Contact number: : +352 26 89 75 11
Special diets: Vegetarian Friendly, Vegan Options, Gluten Free Options

La Tapería - Cafe des bons amis
Location: 120 Rue Albert Unden, Luxembourg City 2652 Luxembourg
Contact number: : +352 621 521 999
Special diets: Vegetarian Friendly

Athena Restaurant Grec

Location: 56 Rue Adolphe Fischer, Luxembourg City 1520 Luxembourg

Contact number: : +352 26 48 37 51

Special diets: Vegetarian Friendly, Vegan Options, Gluten Free Options

Persian FoodBox Hamilius

Location: 21 Rue Aldringen Hamilius City center, Luxembourg City 1118 Luxembourg
Contact number: : +352 28 77 12 77
Special diets: Vegetarian Friendly, Vegan Options, Halal, Gluten Free Options

Dancing Noodles

Location: 9-11 Rue Louvigny, Luxembourg City 1946 Luxembourg
Contact number: : +352 27 29 55 43
Special diets: Vegetarian Friendly

Nirvana Cafe

Location: 1 Avenue de la Gare, Luxembourg City 1611 Luxembourg
Contact number: : +352 691 866 745
Special diets: Vegetarian Friendly, Vegan Options, Gluten Free Options

Cofee and Tea

Golden Bean - The Coffee Experience

Location: 23 Rue Chimay L-1333, Luxembourg City 1333 Luxembourg
Contact number: : +352 26 20 36 60

Lovely place for a coffe on a rainy day

KAALE KAFFI

Location: 9 Rue de la Boucherie, Luxembourg City 1247 Luxembourg

Contact number: : +352 26 26 25 01

Great and Comfy spot for a coffee

Ready

Location: 35 Avenue du Bois, Luxembourg City 1251 Luxembourg

Great and Good place for coffee, tea and also breakfreat

Gruppetto Café

Location: 14A Rue Notre-Dame, Luxembourg City 2240 Luxembourg
Contact number: : +352 26 20 08 04

Great and Good place for coffee, tea and also breakfreat

Casa del Caffé

Location: Avenue de la Porte Neuve N. 11, Luxembourg City 2227 Luxembourg
Contact number: : +352 27 56 54 23

Great and Good place for coffee, tea and also breakfreat

Bars and Pubs

Oscar's Bar

Location: 9 Bisserweg, Luxembourg City 1238 Luxembourg
Contact number: : +352 691 856 874

This is a must visit location. Excellent place of beers

Dipso - the Wine Republic

Location: 4 Rue de la Loge, Luxembourg City 1945 Luxembourg
Contact number: : +352 26 20 14 14

A great place for wine and also a good romatic location for couples.

Sixty Four Bar

Location: 6 Rue du Fort Niedergruenewald Sofitel Luxembourg Europe, Luxembourg City 2226 Luxembourg
Contact number: : +352 43 77 61

Luxury bar with a very great atmosphere

The Tube

Location: 8 Rue Sigefroi, Luxembourg City 2536 Luxembourg
Contact number: : +352 27 28 05 80

A great pub and great selection of local beers.

Octans - A Spirited Bar

Location: 15 Rue du Cure, Luxembourg City 1368 Luxembourg
Contact number: : +352 28 77 47 88

Very good coctail bar with excellent service

SHOPPING

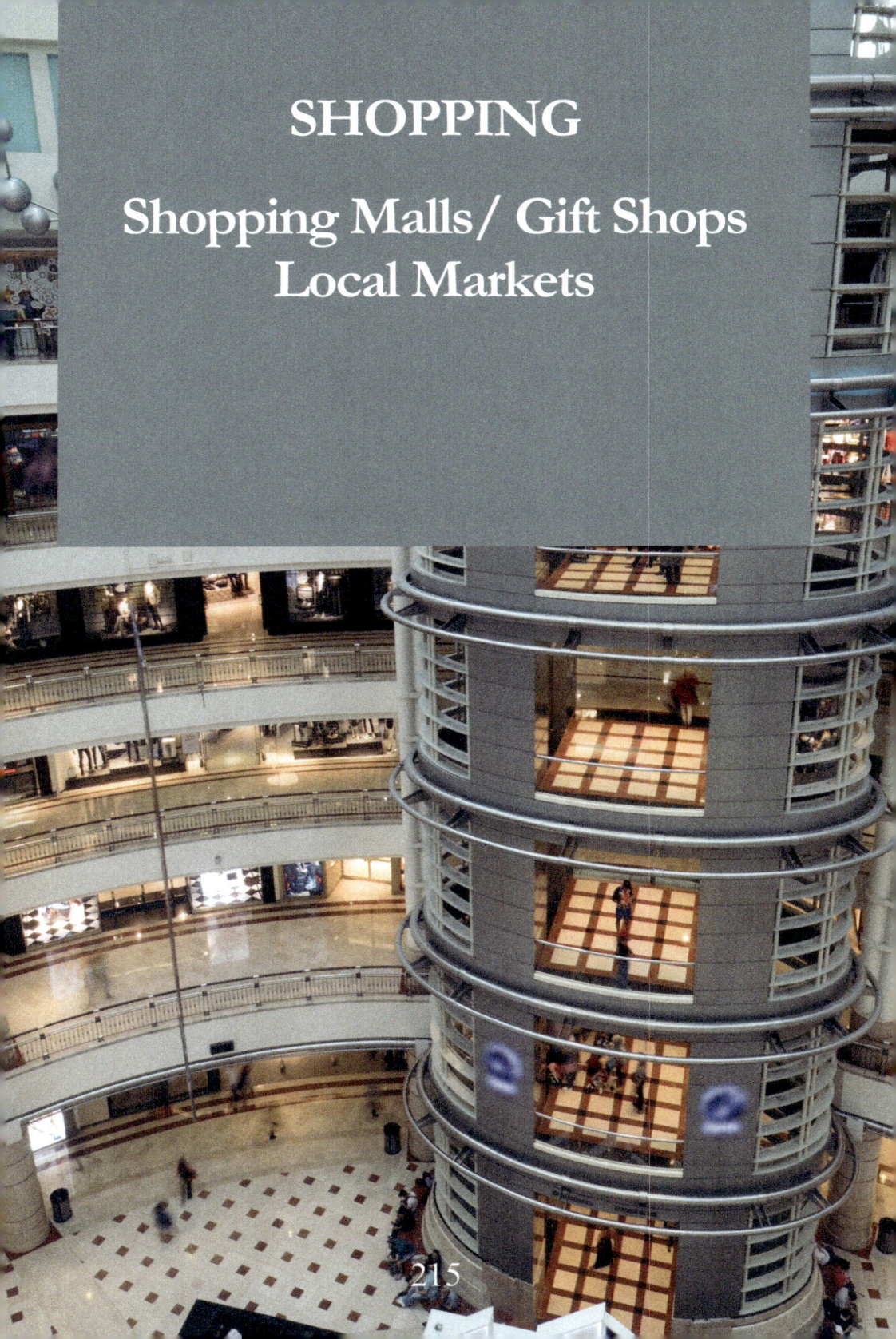

Shopping Malls / Gift Shops
Local Markets

Shopping Malls/ Gift Shops

Massen Shopping Center

Location: 24 Op Der Haart, Wemperhardt 9999 Luxembourg
Contact number: : +352 26 901

Very pleasant and easy to navigate shopping mall.

Knauf Shopping Center Pommerloch

Location: 19 Bastnicherstrooss, Pommerloch 9638 Luxembourg
Contact number: : +352 26 95 47 10

It is a very nice mall that you can find almost everything here.

City Concorde Lifestyle Center
Location: 80 Route de Longwy, Bertrange 8080 Luxembourg
Contact number: : +352 44 93 99 1
Excellent shopping mall with lots of high street brand shops, restaurants, coffee shops, bakeries, butcher, Cora super market & free parking.

Knauf Shopping Center Schmiede

Location: 3 Op d'Schmett Parking gratuit, Huldange 9964 Luxembourg

Contact number: : +352 97 97 33

Great shopping mall with nice varieties of merchandise.

Auchan Kirchberg

Location: 5 Rue Alphonse Weicker, Luxembourg City 2721 Luxembourg

Contact number: : +352 43 77 43 1

This is a nice mall, easy to get to and easy to find whatever you need

Villeroy & Boch

Location: 330 Rue de Rollingergrund, Luxembourg City 2309 Luxembourg

Contact number: : +352 46 82 12 17

This shopping mall has great and excellent choice of high-quality ceramics and glass at a reasonable price it is a must visit.

Local Markets

Antique market

Location: Place d'Armes (côté Square Palach) Place d'Armes
Contact number: : +352 4796 4299

The antique market sells curios collector's items and other treasures.

Market in the city centre

Location: Place Guillaume II L-2346 Luxembourg

The weekly market, also known as "Stater Maart," is held on Place Emile Hamilius and has vendors selling flowers, spices, fresh cheese, handmade jam, and a variety of other artisanal items in addition to fresh fruits and vegetables.

Glacismaart

Location: Glacis Parking L-1528 Champ du Glacis
Contact number: : +352 4796 4299

The Glacismaart sells a wide range of things, including flea markets, flowers, fruits, vegetables, traditional Luxembourgish products, apparel, and decorative items. Opens every third sunday of the month from March to November (excluding August).

Flea market

Location: Place Guillaume II Luxembourg
Contact number: : +352 4796 4299

The flea market is a second-hand market where people can showcase and sell products they no longer require. Not only is the flea market a must-see event for bargain seekers and enthusiasts of unique and peculiar products, but it is also an awesome opportunity to go shopping in the city, since many businesses in the center are open.

Konscht am Gronn

Location: Grund Luxembourg
Website: : www.konschtamgronn.lu

Konscht am Gronn is an open-air gallery situated on the most magnificent bridge in the historic neighborhood Grund. Up to 34 foreign artists display their works in the following areas: Painting and sketching, photography, glass art, ceramics, digital art, works of wood, stone, and metal

EVENTS

Public holidays
National day celebrations
Festivals

HOLIDAYS

1 Jan New Year's Day
1 Apr Easter Monday
1 May Labour Day
9 May Ascension Day
9 May Europe Day
20 May Whit Monday
23 Jun National Day
15 Aug Assumption Day
1 Nov All Saints' Day
25 Dec Christmas Day
26 Dec 2nd Day of Christmas

NATIONAL DAY CELEBRATION

Luxembourg's National Day initially served as a tribute to the Grand Duke's birthday, beginning with Grand Duchess Charlotte's birth date on January 23rd.

However, due to the chilly winter season, the festivities were shifted to the warmer June 23rd, and this date has stuck, even beyond her tenure.

The grand celebration kicks off on June 22nd, the evening before National Day. The capital, Luxembourg City, rings in the event with a formal changing of the guard at the Grand Ducal Palace at about 4 pm.

As night falls, a vibrant torchlight parade winds through the city streets. The capital comes alive, transforming into a massive street party with an array of free live music, DJs, and dance areas for everyone to enjoy.

It's the perfect opportunity to indulge in local treats like sausages, potato pancakes, and a taste of

Luxembourg's beers and wines. Capping off the evening, a spectacular fireworks display lights up the sky from the Adolphe Bridge.

Come National Day on June 23rd, the festivities continue starting at 10 am with an official ceremony.

A salute of guns and a midday military parade down Avenue de la Liberté add to the patriotic spirit. The day's events culminate with the traditional Te Deum service at the Notre Dame Cathedral in the afternoon.

FESTIVALS

Procession of Echternach

Echternach, a town in the east, is famous for its ancient St. Willibrord's Abbey, established in the 7th century by the saint himself and later reaching its peak in the medieval period.

But there's more to this place than just its historic abbey. Echternach is also home to Luxembourg's standout cultural event—the lively Dancing Procession.

This unique tradition unfolds every summer, starting with participants bouncing rhythmically from a bridge over the Sauer River, all the way to St. Willibrord's final resting place inside the basilica. In 2010, UNESCO honored this event as part of the world's Intangible Cultural Heritage.

The procession is a vibrant mix of clergy, abbots, and musicians donned in ceremonial garb, accompanied by throngs of tourists.

It's a sight to behold as they all join in what is the last dance procession of its kind in Europe, cementing its status as one of Luxembourg's most celebrated festivals.

Luxembourg Kizomba Festival

Concentrating on the authentic style of Kizomba, this gathering unites top-notch Kizomba dancers, instructors, and DJs from across the globe.
This sensual dance hails from Angola, and its name in the native tongue translates to 'party.' Kizomba is known for its gentle and romantic vibe, making it a perfect dance for couples of any age to experience. It's a highlight among Luxembourg's music festivals.

This festival starts 28th April to 3rd May
Location: The Box, Exhibition & Congress Centre, Kirchberg

Winter Lights Festival

Luxembourg's Winter Lights Festival is a true gem among its holiday celebrations. Throughout December, the heart of the historic city transforms into a winter wonderland. Imagine meandering through quaint, lantern-lit lanes lined with more than 220 trees, a good number twinkling as Christmas evergreens.

The festive buzz is everywhere, with Christmas markets springing up in the main plazas, brimming with holiday treasures. Both locals and visitors flock to these charming stalls, eager to find unique gifts and seasonal decor. And there's no shortage of entertainment!

The city center comes alive with joyful concerts, enchanting plays, and dazzling circus acts, all adding to the merry vibe of the season.

If you're on the hunt for one-of-a-kind presents, don't miss the souvenir shops that open their doors on Sundays during the festival. They're a treasure trove of festive finds!

Liichtmëssdag Candlemas Day

Much like the US custom of kids going door-to-door for candy on Halloween, Candlemas Day, or Liichtmessdag, is a festive highlight in Luxembourg that coincides with Carnival season.

On the night before St. Blaise's Day, children craft traditional lanterns and parade through their neighborhoods, visiting folks to gather sweets.

This celebration, which is all about 'lighting up' the darkness, is a major hit with the kiddos who eagerly anticipate the treats and sometimes even a little cash they receive on their cheerful rounds.

Schueberfouer

The Schueberfouer stands out as the grandest carnival in the entire region of Greater Luxembourg City located at Glacis, Limpertsberg, an event steeped in tradition that dates back to the time of John the Blind, the noble who ruled as both the Count of Luxembourg and the King of Bohemia starting in 1340.

Nowadays, this celebration is a vibrant showcase of local customs and thrilling amusement rides, including high-speed coasters and towering drop rides that promise a rush for both kids and grown-ups alike.

Just last year, the fair boasted 43 unique rides crafted for the occasion, with 20 designed just for younger visitors, alongside 69 challenging games.

The lively mood of the fair also attracts a host of regional sellers to the festival grounds. Plus, it's a chance for everyone—locals, travelers, and sightseers—to indulge in some exclusive, mouthwatering pastries that can only be found in Luxembourg. It starts 19 August – 7 September

Buergbrennen The Bonfire Festival

The Buergbrennen, also known as the Faaschtefeir or Lint Festival, is a time-honored celebration in Luxembourg that takes place in march on the Sunday following the conclusion of the Carnival season.

This festive event has roots that stretch back to ancient pagan customs, originating thousands of years ago to symbolically bid farewell to winter.

Residents come together to build towering bonfires on hilltops, using a mixture of logs, hay, and branches, all under the watchful eye of the local fire brigade to ensure safety.

When it's time to ignite these buergen, the event is quite the spectacle. Often, the privilege of lighting the fire is given to the newest married couples in town or well-known local figures, who toss in the match amidst great celebration.

Before these impressive bonfires blaze brightly against the night sky, communities frequently partake in torchlit parades that culminate at the site of the fire.

As the flames dance, people gather to enjoy traditional fare, with green bean soup and warming mulled wine being popular choices to complement the lively atmosphere.

Festival OMNI

The most renowned and well-known Luxembourg music festival, this lovely event draws hundreds of locals and international performers to the city.
The festival, which focuses mostly on the blues and jazz genres of music, combines music and festivities, making it a must-attend event, especially during Luxembourg's beautiful summer nights.
Festival OMNI, attracts large numbers of fellow music lovers and aficionados.

Geenzefest

Geenzefest is a stunning festival in Luxembourg that honors the season of blossoming flowers. It's one of the most beautiful events you'll find in the country!

Typically held in May or June, it's when the Oesling area's meadows start to sparkle with the yellow hues of flowering bushes. Imagine the entire scenery draped in a golden hue – it's quite a sight!

During this time, locals come together to put on a show with fancy parades, various exhibits, and a bunch of cultural activities.

The festivities keep up the spirit throughout the entire Whit Weekend. Believe it or not, the festival draws in a crowd of over 10,000 participants!

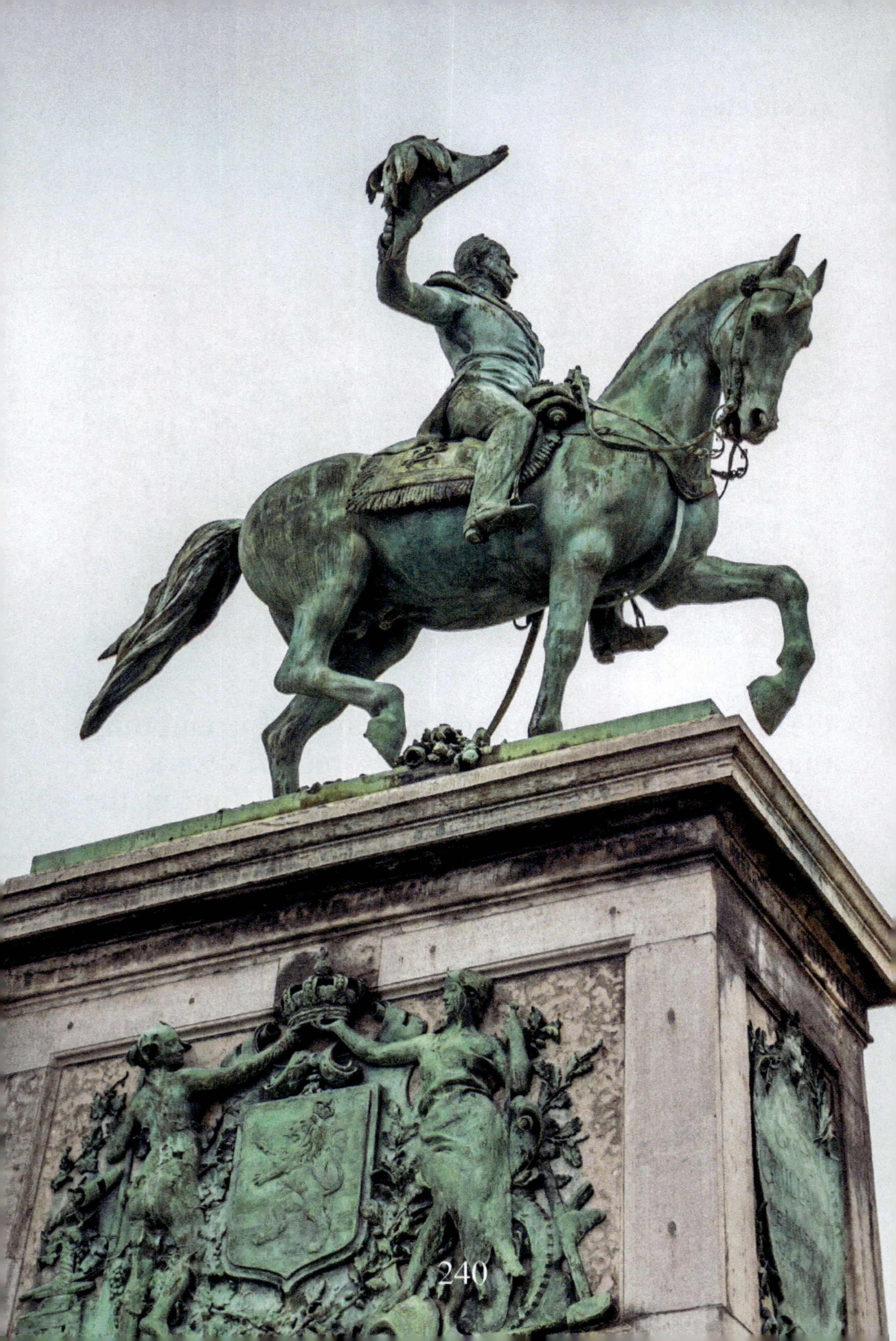

Exploring Luxembourg Map

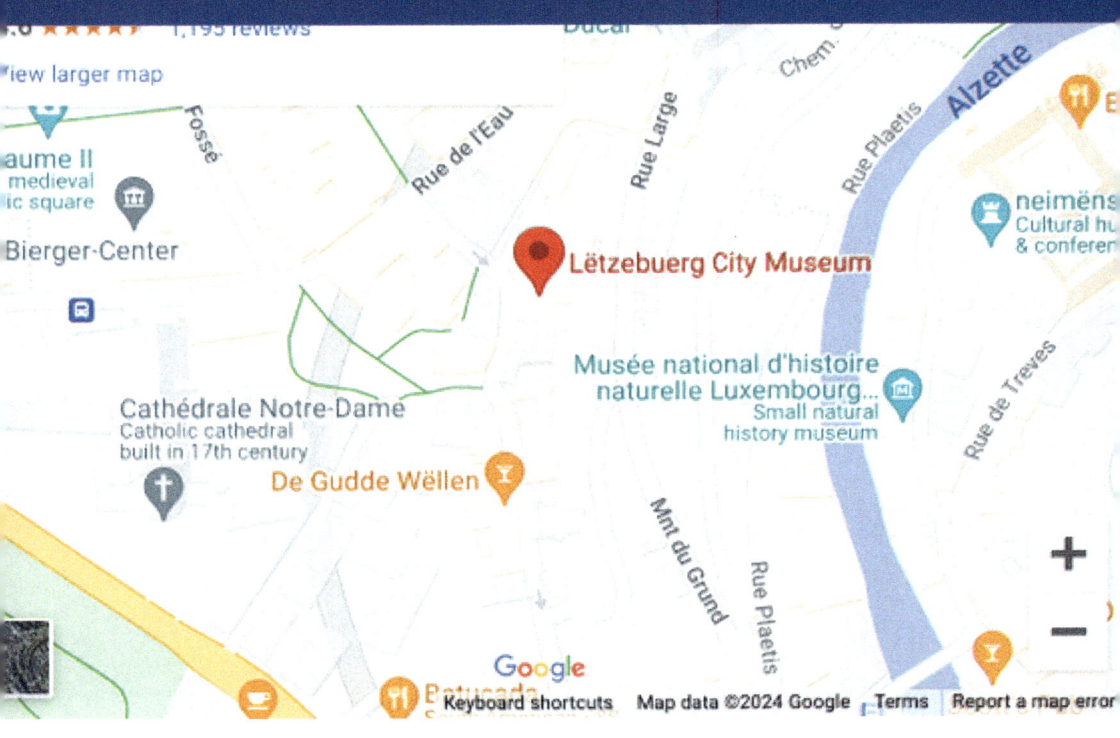

SCAN THE QR CODE

After scanning the QR code you will be directed to your goggle maps app.
There you can type the name of any attractions you want to see, and it will direct you from your current location to the destination.

241

Accomadation Map

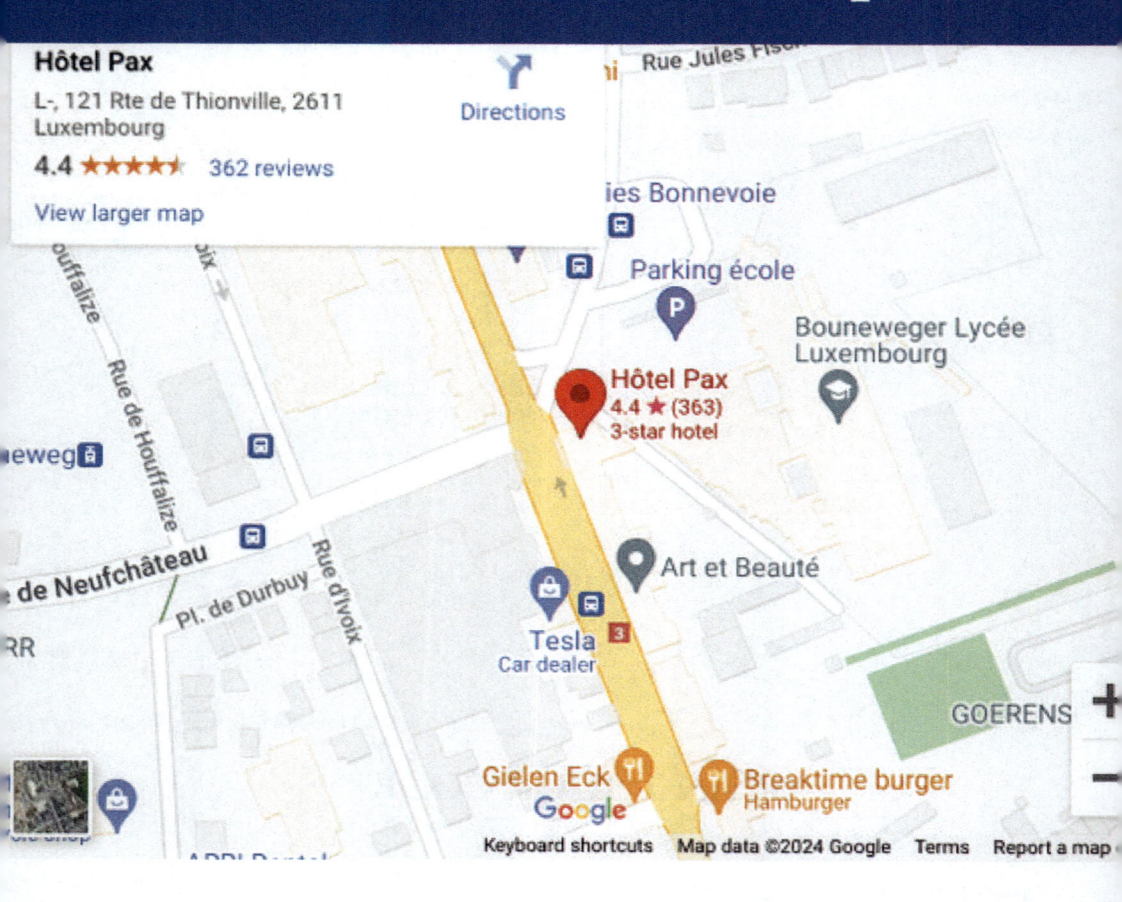

After scanning the QR code you will be directed to your goggle maps app.
There you can type the name of any hotel you want to lodge at, and it will direct you from your current location to the destination.

242

Restaurant Map

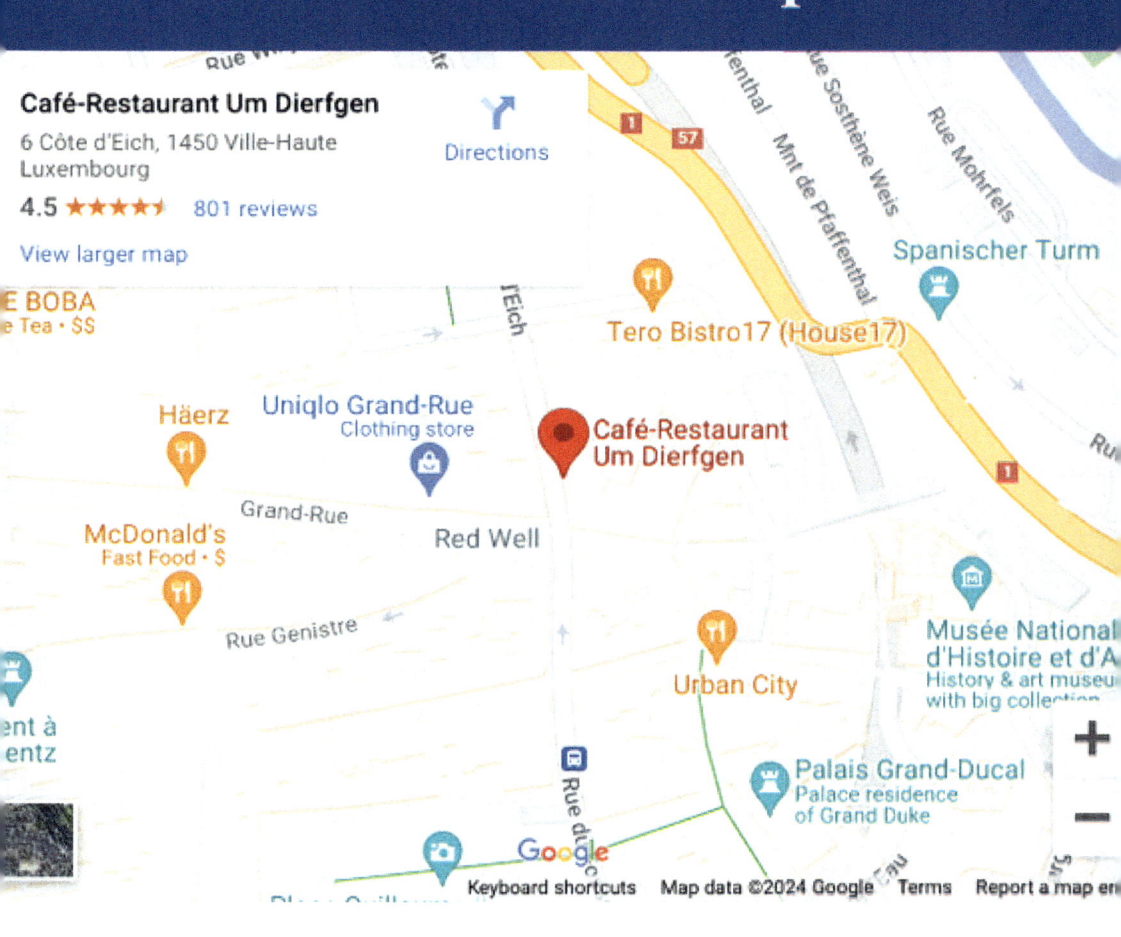

Café-Restaurant Um Dierfgen

6 Côte d'Eich, 1450 Ville-Haute Luxembourg

4.5 ★★★★★ 801 reviews

View larger map

Shopping Map

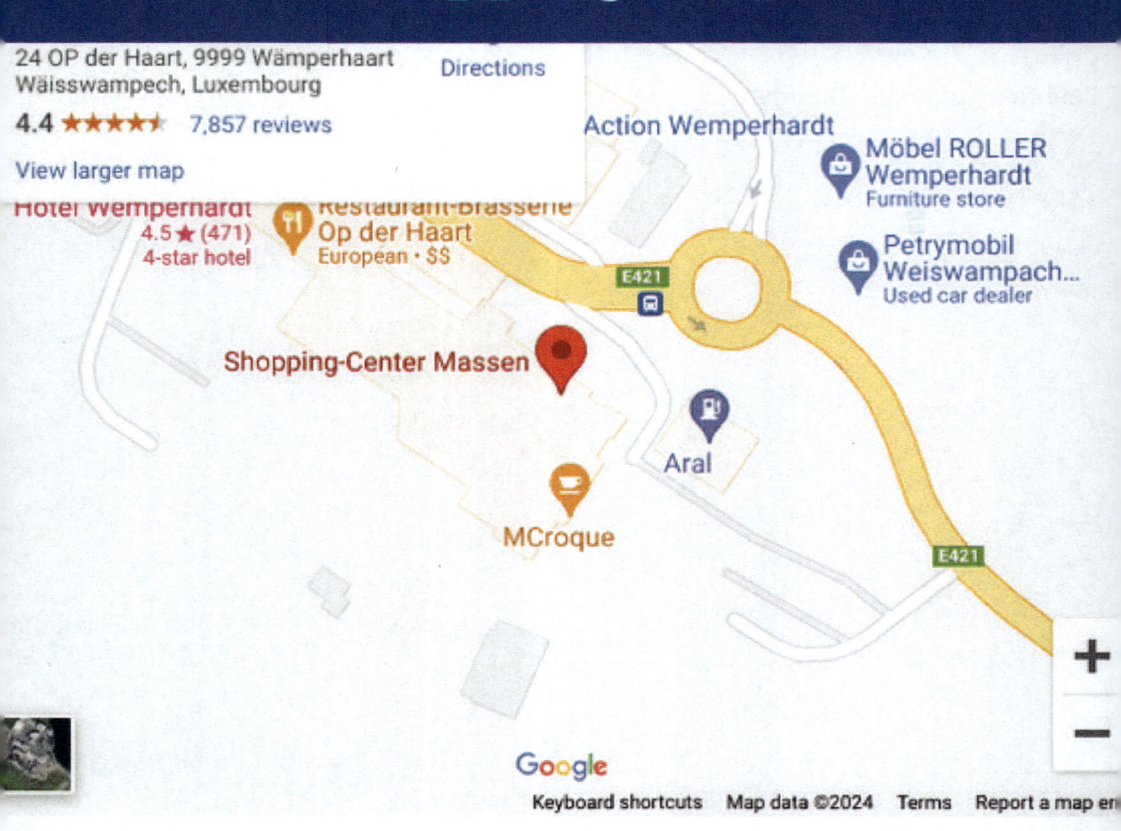

24 OP der Haart, 9999 Wämperhaart Wäisswampech, Luxembourg

Directions

4.4 ★★★★★ 7,857 reviews

View larger map

CONCLUSION

This travel guide has endeavored to capture the spirit of Luxembourg: a country of wonder and discovery. From ancient castles to the Futurescope, from the serene countryside to the busy metropolises, Luxembourg presents to you a canvas of alluring scenes to draw your travel narrative.

As you close this last chapter of this guide, I want to express my gratitude to you, the reader. It is your curiosity and spirit of adventure that makes sharing this adventure possible. Whether you are an experienced traveler or one planning your first voyage, I hope this guide has awoken in you the excitement for Luxembourg and the unpredictability that lies therein.

I'm grateful for the chance to be your guide on this exciting adventure. I hope your journey is packed with awe, happiness, and memories that'll stick with you forever. And don't forget, there's no limit to where your curiosity can take you – consider Luxembourg the starting point of your upcoming epic quest.

Enjoy your trip!

Printed in Great Britain
by Amazon

44366652R00136